TEENAGE RELIGION

TEENAGE RELIGION

An Enquiry into Attitudes and Possibilities
Among British Boys and Girls
in Secondary Modern Schools

HAROLD LOUKES

*Reader in Education in
the University of Oxford*

*Published for the Institute of
Christian Education by*

SCM PRESS LTD
BLOOMSBURY STREET LONDON

NOTE

THIS book contains the results of an enquiry conducted by a group which was appointed by the Study and Research Committee of the Institute of Christian Education, 46 Gordon Square, W.C. 1, with the following terms of reference:

'To enquire into the varying approaches to religious education, during the third and later years, in non-selective secondary Schools.'

Names of members of the study group are listed on page 156.

FIRST PUBLISHED 1961
© SCM PRESS LTD 1961
PRINTED IN HOLLAND BY
DRUKKERIJ HOLLAND N.V., AMSTERDAM

CONTENTS

INTRODUCTION

WHEN boys and girls leave school, it is presumed that they are ready to take responsibility for their own education. They have learnt the 'grammar' of life, the language of word and number, the habits of work and social convention, the skills of hand and eye, and the fundamental values of human relationships; and they are ready to apply their grammar to the experience of life itself. There is still much to learn, but they can decide for themselves how much they will trouble themselves with.

In some fields of knowledge compulsion will continue, and be intensified. Economic pressure will compel the practice of occupational skills; social pressure will continue to mould, for good or ill, their moral attitudes and responses. Much of what they learnt at school will be discovered to be in use in the adult world, and in some directions real progress seems to start when school is left behind. It is a common experience for teachers to meet their old pupils after a couple of years, and find them startlingly advanced, not only in social competence, but in spelling, spoken English, and skill with number. Wherever the school is preparing for what society will demand the teacher can expect his unfinished task to be picked up by other hands.

But there are other fields in which the school is expected to be an innovator, pushing the frontier of the child's mind a little beyond the common practice of adult life, performing a 'silent social revolution' which will meet the forces of counter-revolution as soon as he has left. Schools are expected to make their pupils love good literature when their parents do not read; be discriminating when their parents are being pushed about by advertising; be honest and truthful in a world that makes little effort to be either; to be unselfish in a world that is proud of its organized greed. In the world of values school life represents almost the last chance for many children to learn to love the best; and the school leaver's 'goodbye to all that' is, for many of the riches of the mind and spirit, final.

This is particularly true of religious instruction, laid upon the schools by Act of Parliament, but thereafter laid upon nobody who does not want it. This curious requirement is made by an adult community that has virtually cut itself off from religion: nine tenths have dropped the habit of churchgoing; three quarters never go at all. The reasons for this statutory injunction on the schools to do something society does not do itself have been a puzzle both to agnostics and to Christians. Professor Niblett is probably right in saying that religious instruction is demanded in the Act because 'though a belief in Christianity is not actual in the majority of people, many of them wish it were'. [1]

It is probable, too, that there remains a widespread belief that religion in some way guarantees morals. The adult puts physical exercises behind him, but believes that 'P.E.' was good for his muscles; and so he puts religious exercises behind him, while still feeling that 'R.I.' was good for his moral muscles.

Whatever the motive the charge is there, and many teachers welcome the opportunity of bringing their children into contact with Christian values and providing a standard by which the current values of society can be judged. But if this task is to be attempted it becomes of prime importance to ensure that while they are still at school children can reach a point from which they can go on. Here, more urgently than in mathematics or geography, it is not enough to have acquired a body of 'inert ideas', for while the world can be counted on to lend point to mathematics and geography, however arid, it must be expected merely to see no point in religious lumber; and the young man or woman will dispose of his lumber accordingly. Here, more than anywhere, it is essential that the school leaver should have attained a measure of insight, have seen relevance, and have felt the strain of his own short but vivid experience of real life on the framework of his interpretation of its ultimate meaning. A scientific formula he can tuck away until he needs it in later experiment; a religious formula must become experimental, and must be seen to work, before he leaves; for in this field, he will find men working with other formulae, which, in their way, still work too, but may work for evil. The gospel of 'getting on' makes pragmatic sense to youngsters facing their first job. What sort of sense is made by the 'foolishness of the Cross'?

THE ENQUIRY

This Enquiry is an attempt to answer this question. It was begun

[1] *Education and the Modern Mind* (Faber, 1954), p. 126.

in 1958 when the Institute of Christian Education set up a study group to investigate the present state of religious education in the secondary modern school. The group consisted of a number of heads of modern schools, a member of Her Majesty's Inspectorate, and others with special interests, from the B.B.C., the N.U.T., training colleges, a university, a Diocesan Council, and the Institute of Christian Education itself. [2]

It set out with no intention of using statistical methods, partly because work had already been carried out along those lines [3], partly in the hopes of moving closer to the human situation of the adolescent, to discover what the pupil received from religious instruction, and what went on in his mind. It was not concerned with how much, in terms of sheer fact, the school leaver knows about the Bible, but with how far Christianity makes sense to him, and helps him to make sense of his own human condition. Previous enquiries suggest that the schoolboy retains his biblical knowledge rather better than he retains other knowledge of a comparable kind: his 'scripture' is 'better' than his history. The schoolboy himself, indeed, complains that he knows parts of his Bible too well, to the point of vain repetition. But although a knowledge of the Bible is an essential preliminary to Christian understanding, it does not give understanding until it is seen to be relevant to life. How far is this perceived by boys and girls of fourteen?

Such an enquiry does not lend itself to exact or systematic methods. It might be possible to collect statistics of a sort, by asking children to say whether or not they were able to accept certain propositions, such as 'There is a God.' But such statements would be meaningless. The 'believer' might mean that he believes in 'a sort of a something', in the classic words that so brightened our lives when they emanated from the House of Commons; or he might mean something approaching Job's experience: 'I have heard of thee by the hearing of the ear; but now mine eye seeth thee. Wherefore I abhor myself' (Job 42.5-6). The 'unbeliever' might mean that he sees no purpose in a blind materialist universe; but he might mean, Prometheus-like, that the God he has heard of is too small for his hope of the destiny of man. Among adults, even among members of a Christian congregation, there is no guarantee

[2] See Appendix C.
[3] *Religious Education in Schools,* published for the Institute of Christian Education (SPCK, 1954).

that agreement on propositions means agreement in the way those propositions are held in the depths of the spirit.

What was attempted, therefore, was to make the children speak for themselves, freely and sincerely, and in their own language. This was done in two ways. First, a number of schools were invited to arrange for a class discussion to be recorded; second, children in the same, and in other, schools were asked to comment in writing on some selected statements from the tape-recordings [4].

The recorded discussions were conducted in the normal class, either by a teacher or a visitor. The class was offered the minimum of guidance, and was encouraged to be frank. How frank they were will be apparent from the transcripts which follow. That they were not only frank but sincere is shown by the extent to which different schools made the same points and seemed to think and talk in the same style. What we have here is a record of the way the minds of these boys and girls are working, the confusions they struggle with, and the convictions they have arrived at. And though these confusions and convictions cannot be listed and analysed with any exactness, the record of their discussion conveys to the reader, far better than any tabular statement, the situation in which the children feel themselves placed.

If the capital advantage of recorded discussion is this vividness and first-handedness, its capital disadvantage is that discussion will tend to be carried on exclusively by those who like to talk. On the evidence of the records alone, we should conclude that there is a high degree of interest in religious problems among the young. Teachers who try to promote discussion of poetry or historical judgement or even current affairs will be envious of the way most of these discussions run on, sometimes with excitement and passionate concern. But the records supply no evidence of what was going on in the minds of the boys and girls who did not speak. Is an interest in religion confined to the debaters? Are the silent ones silent in orthodoxy, doers of the deed if not speakers of the word? Or are they simply too bored to take part?

To answer this question, a number of typical quotations was selected and submitted to approximately 500 children for their comment. By this means the silent members could be forced to show their hand, at least to the extent of 'I agree', or 'Yes' or 'No'; and by making everyone contribute, it would be possible to discover how widely a point made in discussion was supported.

[4] See Appendix D.

These papers are not to be thought of as 'questionnaires' so much as 'commentaires' or 'opinionaires'. A good questionnaire is so framed that there can be no reasonable doubt of what is meant, and the answer can be clear and final. But here the object was to obtain not finality but sincerity; to discover, not what glib answer these children would give to a glib question, but how their minds were working. The sharper the question the less would it serve this purpose, for the less would it reach the children's condition. A scalpel is not the instrument for measuring the gripping reflex of a baby's hand.

For this reason it is impossible to use this material to classify children into orthodox and unorthodox. In one or two instances there is virtual unanimity, and where that occurs it is obviously important; but where opinion divides roughly equally, the significance lies not in the numbers saying 'Yes' or 'No', but in the reasons given for the answer. A muddled answer to a questionnaire reveals nothing; a muddled answer on our papers reveals a muddle; and it is in muddles that there lies the focus of the teaching situation.

The account that follows falls into three parts. First is presented a liberal quotation from the tape-recordings. One complete record was selected as typical of them all. It differed from the rest only in being the most comprehensive in the smallest compass. Its main themes are then illustrated by excerpts from other recordings. Second, an analysis is made of the answers to the questionnaires, in which there is no attempt at classification of point of view, but in which the general trends are broadly represented by the frequency of quotation. Finally an attempt is made to interpret the situation, to assess how far it represents a satisfactory or an unsatisfactory achievement for religious education; and to suggest ways in which the problems uncovered may be dealt with.

When the enquiry began, it was directed towards the school leaver in the present organization, aged fourteen. It ignored the grammar school and the technical school, though it took in some of the upper stream children in comprehensive schools. After the material had been collected, the Crowther Report, *15 to 18*, appeared, with its recommendation to proceed at once with plans for raising the leaving age. This proposal, far from lessening the urgency of the problem we are concerned with, increases it, for if these children are to remain at school for another year, it is even more important that the final stages of their religious education should be conducted in an atmosphere of realism and relevance.

The Report points, as we do, to the incompleteness of our present education. 'By leaving school at 15 they are leaving with an essential job unfinished' (para 164), both in general education and in the sphere of religious and moral values, where the leaver is so soon to encounter a contradiction. The Report says (para 268):

> As he enters the outside world, he finds that much that would have been condemned at school or in the family is tolerated and accepted as natural. He discovers that many of the values he has been told he ought to live by seem to be reckoned no more valuable in purchasing power than the currency which Samuel Butler's Erewhonians drew from their Musical Banks. His first reaction may well be disgust either with the apparent cynicism of the world or with what he may now regard as the unreality of school. What will his second reaction be? It is likely to be to fall into line.

The answer to this is not simply 'more school' if the school is indeed unreal; it is more reality in the school. If the extra year is now to come, it must be matched by extra urgency in meeting the human need of children in their present condition. What these children have revealed about the inadequacy of their religious education thus becomes of more significance than ever, and what they reveal of its adequacy becomes a pointer to what should be done in the new opportunity.

CHAPTER ONE

SPEAKING FOR THEMSELVES

Some Extracts from Tape-recordings
of Class Discussions

I · *A Complete Discussion*

*This morning we are going to see if we can put on record some of
the ideas which have been in your minds gradually getting clearer
for a very long time, and we particularly want to find out your
attitude to matters which can be generally called 'religion'. It's an
ugly term, but it covers quite a lot of things. For most people
religion is tied up with Sunday and Church—now let's start just
for a change with Sunday itself. Let me have your reactions, speaking individually, as to what you think Sunday is for.*

'Well Miss, I think it's a day of rest, myself.'

What d'you mean by rest? You don't just go to bed, do you?

'Well, it should be different to all the other days of the week
when you lead an active life. You should keep yourself quiet for
once and rest.'

Well, that's not a bad idea for Sunday—what do you do with it?

'Well, I don't go to Church at all.'

And you?

'Well, I just go out for a walk, or go to the pictures and that's
about it. I take it easy on a Sunday.'

Evelyn, what about you?

'I just take it easy on a Sunday. I go to Church in the evening
occasionally, and go for a walk across the heath, but I just take
it easy.'

*That's three suggestions. Any more ideas on this point? How
many of you do go to the cinema on Sunday? Oh, it's quite a
popular thing, is it? How many of you go out for walks, or cycling?
How many of you just stay at home and read a good book? How
about television on a Sunday afternoon?*

'Yes . . . not very often . . .'

Well now, the matter of Church was raised by one of the girls earlier who goes to Church. Would she mind telling us why she goes? Come on now, anyone who does go to Church, give us some idea of why you go and why you like it.

'Well, I go because I've always been taught to. My father's always been and he takes me with him.'

Now that's very interesting—you've really got a family tradition there—your father goes and takes you with him. That's very nice— now does anyone else go to Church with parents?

'No' (majority).

Do your parents go, even if you don't go with them?

'No' (majority).

So that's the usual picture we're getting, isn't it?

'Well, I don't think you necessarily have to go to Church to pray.'

But do you pray anywhere?

'Yes.'

How many of you were taught as little children to pray or say your prayers?

'Yes' (majority).

I see, quite a number. Anyone definitely not?

'No' (majority).

When you were taught, were you given something to say by heart or what were you taught to do?

'I was taught by the Lord's Prayer.'

'My mother taught me to speak to God as a person, and not just repeat prayers, but I did learn to repeat the Lord's Prayer.'

Was this at night or when?

'Before I went to bed.'

Has anybody else had this experience?

'Yes' (majority).

Now do you continue it in a more grown up way? Do you still pray?

'Sometimes.'

Now then—what are the sometimes that make you pray?

'When we're in trouble.'

When you're worried and when you're in trouble. And who do you direct your prayers to?

'God.'

Those of you who pray, when you pray sincerely, do you feel that you are praying to someone?

'Yes.'

Is your prayer something like a heavenly grocery bill: Please Lord give me, give me, give me . . .?

'Oh no, you don't always pray for God to give you something—sometimes you just pray for him to get you out of trouble, and you couldn't pray to anybody else really.'

'If somebody is ill you pray for them to get better.'

Do you do that? When somebody is ill do you pray for them to get better?

'Yes' (majority).

'You shouldn't just pray if you want something—if you're really sincere.'

I think you're right, Carole. Then what sort of things should make up your prayer? What would be the content of it?

'Well, everyday things I should think, and love in general for everyone you know and for the blind and people like that.'

And do you really try to cover all these things when you pray?

'Yes.'

How about the rest of you? Do you make a habit of prayer about these things that Carole has mentioned?

'Yes . . . Sometimes . . .'

'I think you should pray to thank God for things at times, instead of just asking for them.'

So thanksgiving comes in as well as asking—and praying for other people you think is important, do you?

'Yes.'

Have you ever thought that perhaps God misses you when you don't pray? Have you ever thought of that?

'No.'

'So many people do pray that he wouldn't miss an odd one.'

Yes, I suppose so—or is it? If a mother has ten children, would she notice if a couple didn't come in for a meal?

'Yes.'

Yes—if she really cared she'd notice. Don't you feel that God may be like that? But prayer does bring up this question of God. When you pray do you imagine an actual figure there?

'Yes—No.'

Anybody who really does imagine a figure when she prays?

'More or less, yes, I regard God as a person when I pray to him.'

What does that person look like?

'Very old and very wise.'

Do you really see anything when you think of God—a real person?

'No.'

Do you believe in God?

'Yes.'

But you haven't any kind of visual picture of him?

'I think there's a God, but I don't really think that Jesus was really born—I'm not being horrible—but I don't really think he was ever born.'

You don't believe that Jesus was a historical person—but you believe there is a God? Now what kind of a person do you think this God is—this God that you pray to? What kind of character has he got—kindly?

'Understanding.'

'A friend.'

'Father.'

'Healer.'

'Leader.'

Yes—these are all very positive qualities, aren't they?

'I think that's what makes it so difficult for us to understand God—we know that he's not all positive, and that's what makes it so difficult to understand.'

What does she mean by 'God is not all positive'?

'He can't make everything come out right.'

For example?

'Well, if for instance you say—oh don't let so and so die, and he does die, then you say well, why didn't he save him?'

Well, would you expect God to do as you and I tell him to do?

'Well, if it is something like somebody dying then I think you would really.'

In other words, nobody need ever die if only somebody asked God to make them go on living?

'Well, God knows better than us sometimes, surely?'

Wouldn't you say that that was an answer—when someone dies even if you have prayed for them—well maybe God has a better plan for them? You pray for someone who dies, and when they're buried—but is that the end of the person?

'No.'

'They say you either go to Heaven or Hell—well, I don't believe in two places like that.'

'Some say you come back as an animal . . .'

*Let's sort this out—some of you believe that there's a life
beyond, although you don't know what it is, and some of you
believe that they come back into the world.*

'Yes.'

*Only one girl has said that. Does anyone else believe that they
come back into this world?*

'Yes' (quite a few).

'I think they come back as a different person.'

But you think they might come back as animals.

'I was told when I was little that I might come back as a cat or
a dog, but when you grow up you don't believe that.'

'There was that play on the telly that showed you where you
went when you were dead—*Agony in Heaven*—or hell, it was.
They showed you a short part of what happened when you went
to heaven and then what happened when you went to hell. In heaven
there was all beautiful trees, and in hell there was snakes and so on.'

Did that play convince you at all?

'No, it was more of a comedy play.'

*Would you say that your friends—outside the School, your boy
friends and girl friends and the older people—would you say that
they believe in a life after death?*

'I think most of them do, Miss. I think that everybody believes
in some sort of life after death.'

Do you agree with that statement?

'No' (quite a few).

*Well, have you met people who actually disagree—people who
say that when your body is dead that is the end of you?*

'They don't talk about it.'

*They may not talk about it directly, but it sometimes comes in
as an odd remark, when they have seen a film or a TV show.
Well, this idea of being born back into the world—you would say
that it is pretty common?*

'Yes' (majority).

*Well, that is an oriental idea, not a Christian idea at all. It comes
from the Orient, from the heathen faiths, and it's very interesting
that it is so widely spread. The picture of God in your minds is
pretty blurred, isn't it? One or two of you think of him as a human
figure, but you're not quite clear about it. Somebody said something
about the side of God's character which isn't positive. Would you
understand something if I said the judgement of God?*

'Yes.'

In what way?

'Well, if you pray for something and then you misbehave, and are horrible and cheek your mother, well he just decides that he won't give you what you have been praying for.'

So you think of judgement as a sort of punishment for something you did to your mother?

'I think that God always punishes you in the end.'

What do the rest of you think?

'Well, they say think of God as a person, but I don't think I know of anybody who was perfect, who never told a lie, and you can't really think of him as a person because he is so perfect.'

He's too perfect to be real?

'Yes.'

Well, this idea of judgement then—it doesn't conflict with your ideas about God loving?

'No.'

Well, you've credited God with some nice characteristics, haven't you—he's friendly, and kind, a healer, your leader, etc.—and you fit in with all this that he can judge?

'Yes.'

Do you think that God judges nations as well as individuals?

'Yes' (majority).

Do you believe then that wars are God's judgement on a nation?

'Yes—no' (half and half).

'Wasn't it in a story about Judah that God threatened a famine because the people were so disagreeable?'

In the last chapters of the Bible it does say that God judges a nation for idolatry and so on. You—or people like you—have often asked me why does God allow wars and so on.

'Well, he causes a war when the world is overcrowded! When there are too many people coming into the world, he has to have a war to get rid of some of them.'

'No . . .'

You think war then is a nice way of killing off the surplus population?

'I don't think war is anything to do with God.'

I think God gave man a certain independence and freedom, and that's where wars come in. You see, if God didn't allow men to have wars, then they would have no freedom, and they would have to do all good. It would probably be good for them, but it wouldn't be what they themselves did.

'I think war is just greed. People have some land, and then they want more and more and more and so on. I don't think God has anything to do with war.'

So you feel that man is responsible for his own wars?

'Yes.'

Just like atom bombs and things. You feel that that is our responsibility?

'Yes.'

Do you feel then that it might be better for us if God stopped us doing these things, but he doesn't because of our freedom?

'No, I don't think it would be better, because man wouldn't be able to decide for himself whether he wanted to believe in God or whether he wanted to reject God.'

What do the rest of you think about that?

'Well, I don't agree when they go making atom bombs and dropping them around.'

But it is a human decision to do that—a human being decided to act in that way.

'Yes, but you could say that it isn't fair when God lets one man shoot an arrow and it shoots another man dead, right back through the ages.'

That is the freedom of man—God doesn't particularly want that.

'These people should think when they make these atom bombs that they're only going to kill people.'

Well, it's a very, very grave problem, isn't it?

'Yes, my parents went to some of the Nuclear Disarmament meetings and the man said it was up to some of the younger folk to do something because it would be them who would be living, and it was up to them to stop them being made.'

That's interesting. On the whole do you prefer to be made to be good or do you prefer to be allowed to be bad if you want?

'I'd rather be bad' (majority).

And are you prepared to take the consequences of being bad?

'Yes' (majority).

'Well, it would be ever so dull with everybody being good and cheerful and so on. It changes the routine if somebody is bad once in a while.'

You like a good row do you?

'I like a good argument.'

Well, what do you think then is the value of Evil? You've got vice, and sin, and all sorts of personal failings haven't you? Do you think this is of any real value? Joan?

'Well, I don't think that serious crime is of value, but just the odd row, or a little lie between friends, I think changes the same routine of being good all the time.'

'You have to be a bit cheeky to get on anyway.'

That's interesting—what do you mean by that, Carole?

'Well . . . these film stars and so on, they say lies to get on in the world, and if they didn't say them they wouldn't get on.'

Attract attention in that way, d'you mean?

'Well, you couldn't really call that evil . . .'

What—telling lies?

'Well, not all their get ups and publicity, because that's near enough accepted.'

You would say then that the accepted standard for the people you know is that an occasional lie doesn't matter and a bit of cheek is a good idea?

'It depends on the person.'

'You mustn't be too perfect.'

You mean you mustn't be any better than anybody else? So this is the pattern is it, girls? This thing called the force of public opinion which says you can tell occasional lies, and be cheeky if you can get away with it, draw attention to yourselves somehow— must get on, get plenty of 'lolly'?

'No—you seem to have got the wrong idea of it.'

Well, explain.

'It's horribly difficult—but it would be so monotonous if everybody was good all the time—and sometimes good comes out of evil.'

You mean like when Judas betrayed Jesus Christ, and then he died and out of it has come the whole Christian faith?

'There's a difference between lies—there's black and white lies. A white lie is told to get somebody else out of trouble or to help them, and a black lie is told to get you out of trouble and somebody else into it.'

That's a popular distinction, isn't it? I'm fascinated by this idea that goodness is terribly dull and boring, because what about Jesus Christ?

'That's why I can't believe in him, really.'

So you don't believe in him historically—and you don't believe in him because he is too good?

'Yes.'

'Well, Jesus couldn't have been perfect because that's what they say in the Bible and he was tempted, wasn't he?'

'He was tempted, but he didn't give in to it.'

Well, is that wrong?

'No, everybody is tempted, and that's why I can't understand God. God is never tempted and it never seems to come into God's world even to think of doing anything evil. But at least Jesus did think of doing the wrong thing—he never actually did it, but . . .'

But what did Jesus claim to be? The Son of God, therefore to suffer temptation, so God did know what it is to be tempted. Do you think there is anything about the life of Jesus Christ as you have read it in the Bible which attracts you at all? Or is he just so remote that he makes no contact with you at all?

'There aren't any stories about when he is with the children.'

'Yes, there is.'

'Well, I wasn't taught anything about when he was with the children.'

'I was! He said "Suffer the little children to come unto me." '

'Well, I was only taught about miracles, and I can't believe in those. Turning water into wine—well, that's too far fetched to be believed.'

Doesn't it ever seem to you that maybe they weren't miracles— maybe it was knowledge—maybe he was a very clever man?

'Well, even a clever man couldn't turn water into wine, could he?'

What about the miracles? The girl over here said she found them altogether too far fetched—do any of you find them more or less acceptable?

'Yes some—but not many.'

Which do you find acceptable?

'The blind and the leprosy—I think you can understand those more than the others, really.'

The healing miracles—why those?

'Well, the doctors today can heal all sorts of things with their powers, and it is possible to believe that Jesus had a strange kind of healing power of his own.'

So you feel that is possible?

'But there is faith healing nowadays, isn't there?'

'Yes.'

So faith healing now helps you to understand these miracles? Somebody said there was something she couldn't accept?

'Yes, raising of Lazarus from the dead. It can't be done these days, so why should it have been done then?'

It couldn't be done by a human being.

'Oh, Ma'am, today they heal people by the body, and they are finding out that the mind has a lot to do with the body, and with Jesus, well if they had enough faith in him as a healer, he might have been able to cure them through their minds.'

'Well, there is something in that. These psychiatrists and faith healers seem to have a way of influencing men's minds to help heal their bodies.'

Yes, psychiatry is recognized by doctors now.

'I saw a man hypnotized, and when he was asleep the man told him he wouldn't want to smoke any more, and when he woke up he was offered a cigarette and he didn't want it.'

You see, the miracles were given to us to prove that Jesus Christ was something more than a human being—that he was God. Have you ever considered how all these miracles that no human being could do, like turning water into wine and raising Lazarus from the dead, might have been done to show us in fact that God had come down to earth?

'Well, that's why he did the miracles—to show people that he was God.'

'Well, people can write a book saying that so and so did so and so, but that doesn't mean that it is true.'

Do you think that the Christian Church would exist 2,000 years later if the stories had just been fiction?

'Well, the stories were all written by a variety of people, and they've been translated from one language to another, and somehow they just don't sound right.'

'In Maths and Science today we don't accept anything until it's proved—we say well, if x equals so and so, the so and so must equal x, and we don't accept anything until it is proved.'

How can you prove that the sunset is beautiful by x? How can you prove your mother's love?

'You can't.'

'Well, love isn't like that—you feel love, you can't just say that love is over there.'

What I mean is, there is more than one way of proving something. You can do it in a mathematical way, or you can do it by using your imagination with the sunset, or again with the love of your mother.

'Yes, but it was all such a long time ago. If I hear something,

I like to have it proved, and that's why I don't go to Church or anything like that.'

So what sort of proof are you wanting? You see there is emphatic proof, and scientific proof, and all sorts of proof. That's what I am getting at. I want to know how you can explain the Christian Church 2,000 years later if Jesus never lived?

'Yes, it always fascinates me that when a dictatorship or anything comes up, it only ever seems to be the Church that can withstand it.'

Well, that shows that although it doesn't appeal to you, it does to millions of others, and has done for 2,000 odd years.

'Haven't they supposed to have found a bit of the Cross?'

'How can a cross last all this time without rotting?'

'They're changing things in the Church—when my cousin was christened it was done in an entirely different way to when my sister was.'

'Well, surely the Church must change with time—the priests can't dress the same as they did 2,000 years ago.'

2 · *Belief in the Bible: An Extract*

'But the Bible's not forced to be true, we don't know ourselves that it's true. It could be something that's been made up quite a long time ago since, and it's much better to be able to sit and discuss the things that your teacher's telling you about than to just have to sit and listen, and think oh, well, if the teacher says that's right, surely it must be so. It's much better to be able to discuss it.'

But earlier, Pat, you used the word 'proved', I think. If I remember you correctly, you said 'the Bible has been proved to be true', and then in the same sentence, I think even the same breath you said we don't know it's true. So then if something's proved true, how can it be that you don't know it's true? I know what you mean, but I want you to tell me what you mean.

'It hasn't been proved to me myself.'

It hasn't been proved to you yourself?

'Scientists and people have studied the Bible. It's not been proved to ourselves, to our own personal lives. Nobody's told us who has studied it proper like, only what we've been told by teachers.'

Yes, I think we're getting at a point here which is very important.

That is the point of proof. What is proof? Now we have talked about this before. Anybody any ideas about what is proof? John?

'Well, proof to me is with the five senses, and if I can't see it, or touch or taste or hear it then it really isn't proof to me. But—well—I know I love somebody . . . and I can prove that to myself but I can't prove it to anybody else. Well, say he loves his mother—well I could tell that he loves his mother, and if he didn't like her I'd be able to tell he didn't like her by the way he looked at her and the things he did for her. I think you can tell happiness, and love, and the other abstract things like that.'

And if you took away the evidence of the five physical senses you would say that you couldn't prove anything? Now do you agree with that, Christine? Does anybody disagree with it? Anybody see any reason to disagree with it? Yes, John.'

'Well, somebody in London studies how many, well what the population is in London, and they've proved that the population is well, ten million. Well, that's proof. And it's proof to me, but I haven't proved it myself.'

Well, is it proof to you? You are accepting the word of somebody, aren't you?

'Yes, Sir.'

Now can you take the word of a teacher as proof? Is it proof to you?

'I don't think that a teacher can prove that God is. I think it's up to you to follow on the lines that the teacher gives to find out for yourself if you really believe in God.'

Yes, that's a very good answer. Have you ever known teachers think differently about the subject?

'I think different teachers think in different ways. Some teachers think a lot differently from others, and express their meanings different, and some schoolchildren get mixed up.'

Is that a bad thing?

'No, I think it helps you think more . . . a lot more.'

Then it's a good thing that different people have different ideas about religion?

'I think it makes you think on each one of those lines that they think on.'

Yes, so . . . and what is the advantage of that? First seeing it one way, and then another way . . . wouldn't it be much easier if everyone thought the same thing? Why does Christopher think it's better to have all these different approaches? Yes?

'Because in his idea to choose the one that you think is right. I don't think . . . I don't agree with that because, well, if something is really true, then everybody must believe it.'

3 · *Belief in the Bible: Another Extract*

'Sir, the Bible was written thousands of years ago and nobody knows if it's true or not because it's hard to believe things you have never seen. It's just a story from a book all the time—there's no proof to show that it's true.'

Do you agree you don't know if the Bible's true or not?

'It's all a story, Sir, and there's stories nowadays.'

'Our ancestors were taught the stories from Jesus's disciples. Well, maybe the stories have been exaggerated through the years.'

You mean that you think that bits have been added on? Added on to parts of the Bible about Jesus?

'Yes, I bet if I told a story, and the person I told it to passed it on to someone else and he passed it on and so on then it came back to me, well I bet I wouldn't even recognize my own story.'

Well, if you think that things have been added on, then what do you think is the real truth about Jesus?

'Nobody knows what the truth is. Nobody was there.'

'We read about these miracles—well, we don't know they happened. We weren't there. It may well be a story.'

But you believe he was a good man. If you had to describe him to somebody, how would you describe him?

'Well, Sir, he was a good man, wasn't he? He spent his life healing people and helping them.'

But supposing you were using your own mind to describe him— what would you say? The Bible says he's a good man. What would you say?

'Well, I don't know—I've never seen him, have I?'

Well, what would you say?

'I'm not answering—I'm not going to be caught out.'

'I don't think it can be true what is written in the Bible—it says he is a perfect person, and no one can be perfect.'

'What about the story about Moses—when he was being chased by someone and the water just parted and he walked across? That can't be true. Water can't just part like that and someone walk across.'

'In the Bible it says that Jesus stood on the Sea of Galilee or something—that he just walked on the top of it. Well, that's impossible.'

'Well, I don't believe those things—they're impossible.'

What about the miracles of healing—do you believe in them?

'In Africa witch doctors say that people are going to die within three days—and they do die from fear. Anybody would think that the witch doctors had power over people—when it's just the fear that kills them off. Well, that's probably what happened to Jesus when he cured them.'

So you think it's not really right to talk about Jesus as the Son of God? You think that's an exaggeration?

'It's just imagination.'

'He was just like a minister, and a minister isn't the Son of God, is he?'

Do you think that if Jesus were the Son of God that would explain the miracles?

'If he was the Son of God why did he die on the Cross—why didn't he come down if he had that much power?'

How is it then that we know these things now, and people then didn't?

'Well, it is said that the doctors and people then hadn't the knowledge that they have now, and it could be just the same—he could have taken them all in.'

You think then that science has taught us a good deal—taught us that some things are not true?

'If you had seen Jesus and seen him doing his work, you may possibly have believed it, but you can't believe it now after such a long time.'

You say that seeing is believing, but obviously there have been people who have believed without seeing?

'Well, some people wanted to believe it.'

4 · *The Nature of God: An Extract*

'I don't think God is a person, but more a thought in our minds which we have conjured up, and it has really become true.'

'God must be a kind person who has a great power to command.

I think of him as one of us, but more understanding, and a person who knows everything.'

'God is not visible to man. He is all that is good and kind and he lives amongst us. A God cannot be proved in our minds that is true, so we just have to have faith in him.'

'Well, I think he is a man with long white flowing robes, and hair down to his shoulders, and a long beard.'

'Well, I always used to think of God as a man who sits in a golden throne up above the clouds, and just sits and watches us, and sends his messengers down to us.'

What you said, is that what you used to think?

'I think it now.'

That is what you still think?

'Yes.'

'Well, I think near enough the same as Terence! I think he has a long beard and he sits up above with all the angels round him.'

'I imagine God as a form of superior angel.'

'God is abstract—when people—when—I think we would need a very atomic brain to find out about him, but I think even if the greatest scientist tried to invent something about him, they would not get the real God. Like people call God a he. Well how do we know he is a he? How don't we know he is a she?'

'I was going to say the same.'

Well, say it.

'How do we know that God is a man and not a woman?'

'For all we know the fish in the water and the animals might believe in a God of their own. For all we know they might go to their church services amongst their little families, and they might think of God as an animal like them, and they might think of a fish, you know as a fish like them for a God.'

'Well, I have always thought of God up above the clouds in heaven.'

'I think we only think of God up in heaven, heaven meaning above and hell below, because we think it is a better place above than it is below—not that it really exists, but that is really in a different atmosphere altogether, or everywhere that we could not see.

'I think God is everywhere around us and he is what we say.'

5 · The Nature of God: Another Extract

When you hear this word 'God' what do you think of?

'I think of Jesus and God as one, and if I see a photograph of Jesus I always think of him as God as well.'

When you think of God what do you think of, Pat?

'I think of the Cross and of the Holy Trinity and that Jesus died for us.'

You really mean to say that when someone says the word 'God' to you the Cross comes into your mind?

'I imagine clouds in the sky.'

You imagine clouds. What do you imagine, Joan?

'I imagine him as a presence that can be felt but not seen.'

You have a feeling when someone mentions the word 'God' do you? Anyone else imagine God?

'I imagine God as an angel.'

'I imagine God as a figure. He is in a white robe, and he has all children round him. Just an ordinary looking man.'

You all imagine God as a human being to look at, do you? Although Pat sees a Cross, and someone else has a feeling? Maureen?

'He is always there to protect us, and sometimes you can see him as a sort of spiritual being.'

How can you picture a spiritual being? What does it look like in your mind? If you had to paint it, what would you see?

'Sort of an outline.'

I see, just an outline with nothing inside it. That's interesting isn't it? Where do you think God is?

'I don't know.'

6 · Jesus Christ

Can you tell me, what do you think of Jesus Christ, quite openly and honestly? What comes into your mind when Jesus Christ is mentioned?

'I think Jesus Christ is an example to all of us, the thing that God would really like us to be.'

That we should all be like Jesus?

'He would like us to be.'

God would like us to be like Jesus. Exactly like Jesus?

'Yes, Sir. He would like us to be like Jesus as much as possible.'

So he says be as much like Jesus as you can and everything will be all right. Well, if you read what Jesus says, he says much more than that doesn't he? He says for instance, 'the works that I do, ye shall do also, yea and greater than these shall ye do,' and he gives us very definite instructions. He says for instance 'follow me, take up thy cross'. Yes, John?

'We can't do some of the works he did though.'

Why not?

'We can't perform miracles.'

Why can't we perform miracles? Somebody told me once that men did perform miracles, in medical science these days.

'Well, that's OK but . . .'

What miracles do you mean? Is there any difference between the healings of Jesus and the healings of medical science?

'Well, he did it by the flick of his hand, while the surgeons and whatnot do it with medicines.'

Yes, the big difference as you see it would seem to be the difference of time, wouldn't it? Yes, Valerie?

'It's very difficult for me to believe that God or Jesus just cured people by touching them. In fact I don't believe it, Sir.'

You don't believe that. So the curing the sick of Jesus by miracles you cannot accept at all?

'No, Sir.'

7 · *Heaven and Hell*

When you hear the word heaven or hell what really comes into your mind?

'A fiery place, in my mind.'

When you hear the word heaven what do you think of?

'Glorious sunshine—with all gold seats and that.'

'Somebody told me that heaven is a state of happiness. Is that right?'

Well I am asking you at the moment. I'm not asking myself.

'Well, if there is a heaven, well, where is it?'

'It's here, Sir. It's a place of perfection like, Sir. If you are perfect you are heaven sort of, Sir. Heaven's anywhere, Sir.'

Any other suggestions?

'A place where there ain't no wrong done.'
A place where there isn't any wrong.
'No people hurt by anything that people say or things like that.'
'Another world.'
'Another planet—could be.'
'Well why use another planet, why not stay here on earth, Sir?'
'There's bad going on in earth ain't there?'
'Well there's bad up there, because you've got free will up there haven't you?'
'Do you think God would shut anybody out from heaven, Sir? If they wanted to change their ways, like that thief on the cross who changed his mind. Perhaps the other chap didn't change his mind that we hear of. Perhaps when he got to hell he had wished he had of done and tried to do right then. Do you think God would shut him out then?'
What do you others think about that?
'If he tried to do right in hell do you reckon they would have sent him up to heaven?'
'If he had done right in hell he would have gone to heaven.'
'Do you think you just disappear in hell?'
There is just nothingness, you mean? Anybody else got any ideas about this?
'Well, if you are in heaven you wouldn't remember what you had done on earth would you?'
Why not?
'Because you wouldn't have a brain.'
Why?
'Because your soul hasn't a brain.'
It's not a brain so much. It is memory isn't it?
'Well your soul isn't your memory is it?'
What do you think your soul really is?
'Your character. What kind of a person you are.'

8 · *Is Christianity Worth Dying For?*

'I think you can be good, and honest and true, without religion, but somehow if you have religion it makes you feel happier somehow, and you have something to hold on to, and you don't get afraid so easy.'

So religion is sort of an insurance policy for you, is it?
'No . . .'
It isn't. Something more than that?
'Yes, Sir.'
Tell me, can it be taken away from you?
'No, Sir.'
You can't lose it now? Tell me, Christine, if somebody said to you 'unless you give up all ideas of your religion we will take you out, stand you up against a wall and shoot you'—would you go out and be shot?
'No, Sir.'
So you'd give up your religion?
'Yes, Sir.'
Well, it can't mean an awful lot to you, can it?
'Well, what good would I be shot? I mean I couldn't do much good in the world shot, so I might as well carry on living. I would be good, and honest, just the same.'
Well, is that the purpose? If you really understood the Christian religion, if you are shot, you will still live, won't you?
'I don't really know.'

9 · *Suffering*

Do you think it is a cruel thing that God should let people die?
'If everyone . . . there wouldn't have been enough room in the world for everybody because the population is increasing, so somebody has to die off.'
That is true enough, but Christine, what about somebody who dies young or dies tragically? What is natural is that old people should die and so on, but when a baby dies at birth for example, if a boy of 21 dies, do you think that is terribly unfair on God's part?
'No, because he might have been in misery for the rest of his life.'
'I think that is stupid. Because he might have been a great man, too, he might have been anything. I don't think God, if there—there can't be a God or he wouldn't let them die like that. It's just one of those things that somebody gets killed.'
'Maybe God wants him for something else in heaven.'
Well, now, this is I think the real question. This one about the

unfairness of the world if you are going to believe in God, and in a God of love, so I think we have all probably got something to say about this. Beryl, you haven't said anything yet. Let's hear your voice. Do you think it is unfair that there should be this suffering and fear in the world?

'Yes.'

Now, can we think of different kinds of suffering. I mean a child dies of polio, or a young man was killed in an aeroplane crash. Now is there a difference between these two?

'His body gives way on one part, and on the other part . . . Oh but he has had good health, but something else killed him.'

Yes?

'It is accidental the crash he had in the plane.'

But polio is not accidental?

'No.'

No. We haven't quite got the difference yet, but we are getting warm. What other difference is there between somebody who just dies of polio and a young man who just takes up an aeroplane and crashes? There is one very important difference.

'The chap who has crashed in the aeroplane is killed instantly; well, the person who has got polio isn't. It may be years before he dies.'

Yes, I think that is an important difference, but it isn't the one I am thinking of.

'When a man goes up in the aeroplane he just takes the risk doesn't he, but the other person can't help it.'

Yes, that's it Trevor. That's the real difference. The man chooses to go up in the aeroplane and he chooses to climb a mountain and falls over the edge, or whatever it is. He is using his freedom, isn't he? It's not true of the polio. Now do you think having freedom is a good thing or a bad thing?

'It's a good thing.'

Why?

'Well, you can do what you want to.'

And you would rather have the power of doing what you want to do, even if it means you do wrong things?

'I dunno.'

'You learn by things you do wrong. You learn and then next time you do them right.'

Is that always true?

'Well, in most cases.'

*And you would take the risks, would you? I mean, you realize
that there are risks in giving anybody freedom?*
'Yes, yes.'
And you would take the risks?
'Hmmm.'

10 · *Prayer and Worship: An Extract*

*One of the facts that you were interested in was that boys and girls
often tended to break away from the Church when they leave
school and so on. Is that your view? And why do think that?*

'Well, I don't think they've got anything to look forward to in
the Church. When the preacher goes up into the pulpit all they
preach about is Christ's life—they base the whole sermon on a
piece of Christ's life. That's basic Christianity, granted, but it
doesn't preach about something that's going to happen, something
to look forward to, to give the young people something to look
forward to, to base their religion on. It's too isolated, the Church—
it doesn't come into everyday life. It's a thing on Sunday, a place
to go on Sunday—it's too isolated.'

*Well, what about the worship, say the worship at school assem-
bly? Would you say that that's related to life? To life in school?*

'Well, that's too much everyday. You get used to it. You get it
morning in, morning out—it's just the same routine—it's just the
same—morning music, the lesson, the hymn, the prayers, notices—
out! It's just the same, every morning. They don't have many different prayers, they're only going over the same prayers—'Will you
please turn to page 22.' The same piece of piano music about three
or four days running. They don't ring the changes. Nobody listens
to the reading. We have a laugh at the reader.'

*Well, I was going to say do you think the school assembly is a
good beginning to the day? Would you rather be without it?*

'No, no, not without it. Not for me personally, but I think a lot
of people would. A few people I'm meaning, but in a school with
800 it's definitely 90% without effect. Nobody in this school I
mean is really sincere about prayers.'

Not sincere enough? Is that because the prayers aren't the sort they can be sincere about? Is that because the prayers aren't related to life again, or what?

'I think it is, yes. You see they're already out of the book and you have to just—you see, I doubt if many people in this school really believe in Christ.'

11 · *Prayer and Worship: Another Extract*

About our morning assembly—do you enjoy it?

'Yes, I do the singing, Miss. I've always loved singing, and if you've any trouble you can pray, because each day we can pray for a different thing and that, and if you think you've done wrong and that . . .'

Who else agrees? Yes, Janet?

'Yes, Miss, and the school comes together at the beginning of the day and you are always together and it helps you all through the day.'

Now do you think that when you've left school—you won't know this yet—but do you think that you will miss having this act of worship first thing in the morning?

'Yes, I do, Miss, I think it starts the day off properly.'

So what will you have to do about it?

'Pray to yourself before you get up in the morning.'

Sometimes you may not have time to pray first thing in the morning when you're late for work.

'You can still go to Church or Sunday School.'

Yes, you see I don't think we should take the place of Church or Sunday School. It's something extra, isn't it. But I think you'll find you'll miss it very much indeed when you haven't got to go to it. I hope you will, anyway.

'I don't think I would miss it.'

You don't? You just come because you have to?

'Yes.'

'I like it when we pray for the sick. I think that something really happens when you pray for the sick people and the old people.'

What about when we pray for the school?

'Well yes, but I prefer to pray for young people and the old people.'

You think it's valuable, or wouldn't you miss it?
'No, I don't really think I would.'
What do you think, Lorraine?
'Well, I wouldn't really, I feel the same as Marion.'
What do you think?
'Well, I don't know what to say.'
I think we'll have a week when I shall say—only those who want to come to assembly come, and those who don't can stay in the classroom. Now how many of you would come? Right, hands down. That's almost everybody, so that means you didn't really mean what you said.

12 · *Scripture in School*

What do you think about the Scripture you have in school? What use do you think it will be, or will not be?

'Well, when we have Scripture it's like the teacher dictating to the class—I think it should not be so much "what Christ is" and "what Christ did" but more of a discussion.'

'We used to keep going back over the same things and they'd flog the same old things to death. It was all about the Bible and not about Christianity and its effects. I don't think Christianity should be forced on people. Now we have one hour lesson a week and that's in the form of a discussion, and I think more people should take notice if it's a discussion. But well, in our form you get three or four people taking part and talking and the rest . . . well, it's never come to any use.'

'The ideal place to discuss religion is at a party where everybody is talking and discussing their views.'

'Well, at a party you are not afraid to say what you feel, but in a class . . .'

'Well, in a class one day I said more for argument's sake than anything else, I said that Joshua could stop the water-fall if he really wanted to, and nobody said anything at all. They just sat there dumb. I don't think you can hope to get any views at all in a class.'

Well, is it an interesting subject or not?

'Yes, it's a very controversial subject. But Scripture lessons are totally boring.'

'One is inclined to sit back and let the teacher do the work.'

In what way do you think that R.I. is important?

'Because R.I. is spiritual. Maths—well, if we did Maths all day we'd be robots.'

'It makes you think for yourself.'

'It gives you a background of the Bible.'

You wouldn't do away with R.I.?

'No.'

So you just want to change it?

'Yes, it needs some radical changes.'

CHAPTER TWO

JUDGING FOR THEMSELVES

The Pupils Comment on Problems
Raised in Discussion [1]

I · *Belief in Creation*

Well, it could be true that God made the world, Miss, but it's not proved, is it? Nobody stood there and watched him, so we don't know if he did it or not.

Here is a statement packed with confusion but full of provocation and promise. The sophisticated reader would try to deal with it by clearing up the confusions: the semantic confusion that springs from a failure to recognize the present tense in 'God made the world'; the theological confusion that sees the personality of God as limited by the forms of human personality; and the logical confusions that spring from a failure to differentiate different kinds of proof. But the unsophisticated reader sees none of this, and accepts the statement as a challenge to take sides.

It is here that it is so full of promise, for it is sufficiently challenging to make the orthodox believers bridle, the orthodox disbelievers cheer, and the thinkers and seekers to set out something of their difficulty.

Our believers expressed themselves in flat affirmatives.

You should believe in God and not have to have everything proved.

I believe that God created the world and everything that is in it.

The disbelievers are equally clear.

Science has satisfied me that the creation of the world and all the other similar objects in the universe was purely natural without any spiritual help of any sort.

I think that it is a lot of Hill Billi nonsens that is no true.

[1] See Appendix D for the method followed.

I think the world was a scientific accident and was not created by God.

These two groups, who have settled the matter one way or the other, are small beside the many who are still thinking, aware that there is a problem, aware of mystery, and ready to worry at it. Some of them are perhaps too daunted by the mystery to have much hope of making progress:

Nobody knows who or what made the world because it was before man's time.

Others are anxious about their own capacity for the struggle:

I can find no answer clear enough in my mind to write down on paper.

I feel as if it is one of my problems yet to solve and if I did attempt it I would probably be going round in circles and this would confuse me as well as you more.

More interesting are the various forms of attempt to provide an intelligible answer, or at least an intelligible way out of the problem. Some of these are no more than a rationalization of defeat. Not only is the *act* of creation too difficult to cope with: the very *existence* of creation may be illusion. At first sight this may seem a curiously abstruse notion for fourteen-year-olds to entertain, but it was not infrequent.

Of course it is not proved, for how could anyone stand there and watch him make the world, when the world does not exist. In my opinion the world is more of a thought in God.

I don't think God made the world. I don't even think there's a world at all. I believe we just think it's a world. In other words the world is thought, everything is thought. If you look at it any other way that I can think of you come to a 'dead end'.

In contrast to these subjective nihilists, there are those who are sure that the scientists have an answer, even if they themselves are not sure what the answer is.

I do not believe that anything made the world I believe that it is just like stars made up of gasses which collect together because of magmetism of gravity.

Inposaedul. Scinstes say it comes of anther planit.

I believe God made us and all animals, but I dont really believe that he made the earth. For scientist have found out that the earth was a ball of fire which had fallen from the sun. I think that the earth developed and made its self and as it called of it turned into country side's.

Still others are worried by the apparent necessity of choosing between two views of creation, and wish one 'side' or the other would settle it once and for all.

Astronomers tell us that the world was once a part of the sun and that it broke away. Then you read in the Bible that God made the world, some people must get dreadfully muddled, and I would like to know whether the astronomers are Christians, as they seem to me to make the Bible just like any other story which has been made up.

What is missing from all these statements is the realization that they are discussing, not an academic question about what happened when nobody was watching, but an immediate problem in which everyone is involved, and about which there is some sort of evidence awaiting our interpretation. To say 'God made the world' is really to say, 'The world is made, *intended*': and to affirm or to deny it is to make a statement about the meaning or meaningless of human life. Albert Camus has said that after all it does not much matter whether the earth goes round the sun or the sun round the earth, the only serious question being whether, either way, our life is worth living. And the question of how the world was made, whether by 'gases magnetized by gravity' or by 'scientific accident', though obviously a question of great interest, is nothing beside the question of whether or not the world looks 'intended'.

A few children approach this concept:

God must have made the world because there was nobody else to make it.

There is a world, and it had to be made by somebody, so why not God?

If God did not create the world, who did?

The world has been here for thousands of year, but there must have been a beginng and someone must have started that beginng, so why not God?

If God did *not* make the world then who on *earth* did, somebody must have made all the world, and we call him God, and worship him.

And a very few show signs of awareness that the problem of meaning is different from the problem of physical causation:

> God put a living organism into the world after it had cooled down.

By itself, this will not do as a solution. Even the Genesis myth regards matter and spirit as integrally related, and parts of the same process of creation; but the boy who wrote this is at least aware of two levels to the problem, and is open to the two levels of argument on which it must be discussed.

In evaluating these responses we must bear in mind the effect of the remark on which they were asked to comment. It was calculated to divide the contented believers from the contented disbelievers, but it offered no help to the thinkers on either side. In the circumstances, the answers provide an exciting challenge, for the number of children who conveyed the impression that there was more to be said, even if they were not themselves ready to say it, was very large. And the argumentative tone of the 'settled', together with the thoughtful, serious tone of the 'unsettled', indicates a readiness to pursue the matter further.

2 · *Belief in the Bible*

> The Bible's not forced to be true, we don't know ourselves that it's true.
> It could be something that's been made up quite a long time ago since.

Here is the same desire for proof: a suspicion that the Bible is concerned only with a distant past, and that what it says cannot be relevant to or judged by, our contemporary experience.

As we should expect, the comments fall into similar groups. We have the same believers, untroubled by doubt.

> The Bible isn't forced to be true but I still think that every word in the Bible IS. Some people like to think the hard way like the Speaker.

> I believe the Bible is true, because I don't think anyone could be clever enough to make up the kind of stories that are in the Bible.

> There are many proofs that the Bible is true, but even if we did not have these proofs, there are still many, many people who would

believe. After all, an old tune or dancing phase will die out after ten or twenty years. But the Bible, and the news it gives, is spreading, day by day. Some of the material in the Bible is thousands of years old.

> I disagree with this remark. I believe who ever wrote the Bible was guided by God to write the truth just as it happened.

We have the same confident unbelievers.

> The Bible is just a collection of tales and song and poetry made up by some people to explain the world in my opinion.

> I think that the bible's not forced to be true because realy we dont know that it's true, we and many people before us have been made to believe it but realy we have been brought up to church and to read the bible. I myself think that the bible could have been writen by someone some time ago made into stories like legens and myths.

> It has been proved to bee wrong.

> ther is a lot of rubis in it techers abmit ther is so that I do not think that it is true.

We have also the same group of thinkers, who are prepared to examine the issues. Here, of course, they have an easier way out of their difficulty, for it is well within their competence to perceive that, even on the level of truth they are discussing, the Bible may be variable in its value. So while a few give up the attempt:

> It could but was it? I was not there so I do not know. Are any stories true? As we grow up we realise that Father Christmas and fairies were unreal, so why not the Bible?

others are still serious:

> The Bible is something that could have been made up, but I believe parts of it are true, and I reconed that some is just made up to make it sound good.

Others are ready to admit that parts may have been 'made up', but not to dismiss even them as irrelevant:

> I think most of the bible is true parhaps some of the stories where made up but not just to fill the bible up, but the stories I think are made up are the ones with morale behind them.

> The Bible must be either totally true or partly true, or the people that have believed it wouldnt. People would not make up such a thing because there would be no point to it.

Some take the next step from this position, and affirm the right to believe what it suits them to believe:

> It is up to oneself which stories or accounts one believes or disbelieves in the Bible.

> Even though I have been brought up to believe in God and the Bible I still believe it in my own way.

Many children, however, are dimly aware that the discrimination between parts of the Bible must be made on principle, and that some of the difficulty of the Bible may be resolved by rational means. Some are aware that the Bible is a library from many authors, and not merely a book from one man.

> The Bible as you go through it is made up of different 'books' as they're called, and these 'books' are put together to make one large book. Different persons have written these 'books' and they all seem to end up with the same ending and point although they're not the same story. I think a book such as the Bible would be too great a task to make up. The stories are true to life and could have been possible. Of course the above statement could be right as there are certain things written that are hard to believe, like the part where the man and woman were turned to pillars of salt.

Others attribute some of the difficulty to problems of translation.

> I think that the Bible basicly is true. But the Bible has been translated from language to language so many times that parts of it have been misinturprided.

> I think that most of it is true, but most of it is old fashioned; As it has been translated some of it has lost its original meaning.

Some point to the error that creeps in from oral tradition.

> Not all of the Bible is true, for it is not an eye-witness account of things but of what people believed did happen. Before many stories in the Bible were ever written, they were told from one generation to another, thus missing and adding different actions or what they thought had happened.

The recent work of the archaeologists has made its impact, as in this cautiously worded statement:

> Some of the Old Testament is not very clear, or difficult to believe, but possibly in the latter place it was just symbolic. Archeologists have probed into this matter and discovered accounts agreeing with

those in the Old Testament. I believe entirely in the New Testament, which contains the Christian doctrine and points Christ out as universal for all to come and believe in him.

The comments on the Bible tend to be longer and more fluent than those on the idea of creation. This is what we should expect, for the problem is more concrete, more manageable, and more open to a compromise solution. And here is one of the important elements in the situation, that these children of fourteen are, for the most part, anxious to find a solution. What they find is usually superficial, and will need to be replaced later; but the effort to shape it suggests that the children feel the need of some resolution of tension if they are to live at peace with themselves. They are most of them aware of mystery, and are honest enough to seek an explanation that will meet the genuine difficulties in the situation. This honesty is not the prerogative of either side of the argument. A scientific rationalist feels he must explain why Christians hold their curious beliefs:

> Nobody has any proof that God made the world. People like to think that he did just because they can't think of any other way the world was created.

At the same time, the Christian orthodox make their efforts to distinguish between meaning and myth:

> I believe that god was alive when the world was formed but not that he actually made it especcially not in six days anyway. I think it would be impossible for one man to build the whole world.

At the same time, it must be admitted that none of these efforts is successful. Fourteen is too young to expect much insight into a point of view that one does not wholly accept, or to feel very vividly the difficulties inherent in one's own point of view. In this respect, the Christians emerge curiously better than the rationalists, for they seem more able to hold to what they believe and understand the difficulties of it. The rationalists, indeed, have very little except confidence. They know less about the scientific myth than the Christians know of theirs; and the objection made to religious instruction in childhood, that it involves so much unlearning in later life, is at least as applicable to the spreading of general scientific concepts. 'God made the world' is still valid even after the escape from anthropomorphism; but 'gases magnetized by gravity' will need radical replacement. And while the Christians have heard of the archaeologists, the scientists have not heard of Fred Hoyle.

Here, then, from our first question we may derive some encouragement for the teacher of Scripture. Our children are interested, are thinking for themselves, and are mentally prepared to deal with the problems that arise.

3 · *The Character of God*

I've always imagined God as an old man with long hair and a beard, wearing white robes, with a nice calm face and that.

Here is the vision of God as we should expect it to be expressed by a child under the influence of Old Testament language and Christian art. We should hope that the adolescent would find it inadequate: that the believers would see that there is more to be said; that the unbelievers would realize that it is something other than this that they have chosen to reject.

Most of our comments reveal that the real issue has not been faced. The orthodox are wildly confused, and fall back on mere words or statements too vague to carry meaning.

> God is, God the Father, God the Son, and God the Holy Ghost.

> I imagined Him as a person with three heads, the Father the Son, and the Holy Ghost. As the Bible says, Three in One.

Many agree that God is good, kind and loving.

> As long as we believe that there is a God who loves and takes care of each one of us, I do not think it matters how we imagine Him.

> I imagine God as a good spirit, with no faults at all, who symbolizes love, honesty and faith.

> To my mind he is wonderful power, Divine Love.

> I imagine God as been a Good, kind, Gentle, loving man.

The biblical note of God's transcendent majesty and righteousness is hard to find. Some are conscious of God's supreme power.

> God is a being of great power, above mine or anybody else's imagination.

God must be so powerful that I imagine him as some strong, big man, seated in the sky, attended by many angels.

Here, indeed, we have a sense of God's glory.

A Christian would never think of the eternal king as an old man.

God or Jehovah is a spirit and no man has seen him, but in the scriptures it says that all the jewels in the world would not near match his glory.

Such views, however, are exceptional, and we look almost in vain for some hint of God's hatred of evil, except in the policeman view so tempting to the young:

God is fair because if people do wrong he always punishes them. If we do something wrong he knows.

Of those who profess a belief in God, almost half agree that God is spirit, and therefore without a physical body, and unseen.

I can't imagine what God looks like, because he is a spirit and no one has ever seen him.

I think of God as something like a spirit that has complete control of us and influences people who live on the earth.

I do not agree with this because if God is a spirit, how come he has got a body.

God is a spirit, I think this, because how would he be able to be more than one place at once.

Yet we are reminded that to teach that God is a spirit has its own pitfalls.

I imagine him as a sought of Ghost or spirit.

One or two express their belief in God's spiritual nature rather differently:

Sometimes I imagine him as a great shining light.

As we grow older we think of God as a voice who watches all.

About one in three appears to think of God in anthropomorphic terms. It must be recognized that to say 'I imagine God as' is not the same as to say 'I believe God to be'. Nevertheless few are careful to distinguish between their imaginings and their beliefs.

I imagine God as an old man with longish white hair and a nice clean shaven face, with blue eyes like my Grandfather's. God must of been a good man to of been able to create the world, and I believe he is really just like any other middle aged man.

Descriptions of God's appearance vary, 'young', 'old', 'with a beard', 'without a beard', 'wearing white robes', 'a giant'. Mostly he is thought of as old, and two explain this as follows:

I always think that God must have been fairly old because he is supposed to be so knolowgible.

I should imagine he was like that because he lived such a long life.

The influence of the father-figure is apparent in

I have imagined God as a father with a sort of father's face, about thirty-five years old.

To some God's imagined appearance is indicative of his character.

I imagine him to have clumsly looking hands, which always felt very gentle.

I've always imagined God with the sort of face that calms you straitaway when you look into it.

I imagine God not always with a calm face, because when he worries about things his face wouldn't be calm.

He has a old wise face, the most lovest eyes twincling a little, and laughing at our little arrers.

I've always imagined him with a determined expression on his face.

The main emphasis is on God's kindness rather than on his righteousness. One child appears to regard God as a somewhat pathetic object of pity.

I believe God to look like this. I always have and always will, maybe that is why I always feel terribly sorry for old men, especially if they have beards and are poor.

Another speaks of his 'sad face'. We are a long way here from God the Father Almighty of the Bible and the Church. And so is the child who says that God reminds him of Neptune, 'the only difference being that God is in Heaven and Neptune in the sea.'

It is not surprising that there is some confusion between God and Jesus.

I always thought that God and Jesus were the same person.

As a result some anthropomorphic descriptions of God seem to relate to the historical person of Jesus Christ.

I believe that God was a middle-aged person, very kind, had a long beard and extremely kind and gentle to small children.

No, I don't think that is true because its said in the bible that Jesus was 33 years of age when he died.

It is a far cry from such naive anthropomorphism to the doctrine of God's immanence. The rarity of this view makes it worthy of note.

When I was young, I thought that God was an old man, but now I think he is part of you.

I think that God is the soul of every person, because that is pure and when we die the soul leaves us.

I think that God is not physical but a spirit in the minds of men.

One child finds that this conception brings its own problems:

I believe that God is not a physical thing, but other men's thoughts (their good thoughts) their bad ones being the devil. The one thing that puzzles me is that he sent his Son and the Son usually looks like the father.

Terminology which is properly used by theologians may create quite unexpected difficulties for the simple and literal-minded.

Some are prepared to assert a belief in the existence of God, but cannot imagine him.

I haven't imagined him at all. All I know is that there must be Someone, but who I don't know.

You cannot say what God is, because nobody's seen Him.

I can't imagine what God looks like at all.

I have never thought of him as a man with long hair, in fact I don't think many people think about him at all.

One child is content to say

I believe in god in one way or a nuther.

The sceptics were not numerous, making up approximately a fifth of the group. Those whom we may regard as agnostic questioned the reality of God, asking for proof, and not prepared to accept blindly what they had been taught.

People imagine God as an old man because that is what they have been told he's like. But who can prove it?

Different people imagine God in lots of different ways ... but we cannot be sure.

If god was to show his self to us just once more people would believe in him.

And the outright unbelievers argued that God was a figment of man's imagination, a convenient explanation for things men do not understand, a projection of man's need for something to worship.

I think God is a figurehead, that someone created to worship.

I think God is an imageanry thing in men's minds for them to fall back on when they come across something they don't understand, or when they are beaten by something.

I do not believe there is a God. Where could he be: he could not be in space, for all we know space goes on and on.

God could be the result of pagan ceremonys many millions of years ago, when the people of that time had great faith in their prayers, and created him to receive them.

I don't think there is any one up there, it is just what we have been made to believe.

4 · *Belief in Jesus Christ*

I think Jesus Christ was just an ordinary man—after all, he came down in the form of a man. I think he was just a very clever man that came on earth before his time, because nowadays by an operation you can make blind people see again.

This remark invites our commentators to assume that Jesus existed, but to question whether he was in any significant way different from other men, directing attention specifically to the problem of miracle rather than to his moral and spiritual insight. The great majority conformed to this pattern. About a tenth questioned the assumption, classing the story of Jesus with the other legends they so confidently rejected; while the remainder distributed themselves fairly evenly between an orthodox, but not very profound, belief in the divinity of Christ and a critical humanism that sought to explain away the supernatural element.

The orthodox statements regard Jesus as the Son of God, sent to save us from our sins, and to show us how to live. His miracles distinguish him from other men. He is the Creator, God come to earth. For most of this group the miracles are decisive. The suggestion had been made that Jesus was really no different from the modern surgeon who can make the blind see, but this is not accepted.

> Jesus showed by his miracles that he was an extraordinary man, and even now surgeons cannot make blind people see again just by saying 'see', and an ordinary man cannot make two loaves and two fishes feed 5,000 people.

> Jesus Christ was the Son of God, who was able to make people well because of the power sent from God through him. Jesus healed by the touch of his hand, not by anaesthetic and surgical equipment.

One quotes St Paul:

> How could an ordinary sinful man heal people and be so good and do no wrong, for the Bible says that 'All men have sinned and come short of the glory of God'?

Some accept the paradox of the Incarnation and assert that Jesus was both man and the Son of God.

> I believe that Jesus Christ was an ordinary man in some ways, but if he was how could he rise from the dead. I believe also that Jesus was the Son of God given to Mary in the form of an ordinary child.

> God came to the earth in the form of Jesus Christ, an ordinary man, to show us how we should live. So in a way he was an ordinary man.

> Of course Jesus came to earth in the form of a man, what else could he of come as . . . Jesus may have been in man's form, but he was more in spiritual being.

Three further quotations must suffice to indicate beliefs concerning the purpose of Christ's coming.

God wanted to show his love for his creation by sending his son in the form of a man to live with them and show them what God was like.

Jesus Christ was no ordinary person when he came into the world to die for us in order that we might be saved.

He was sent to us to forgive our sins as we say.

One 'orthodox' statement echoes Tertullian's famous *Credo quia impossibile*.

I think it is impossible, but I believe in a way.

Those who may be designated 'near orthodox' are also impressed by the miracles.

Jesus Christ could not have been an ordinary man, because people have tried to turn water into wine and have not succeeded.

When Jesus healed the blind, he didn't have to operate on them.

Jesus Christ was a man who used to heal people with a touch of his hand or a word from his lips. And not by performing an operation such as is done to-day.

One suggests that the power to heal by faith ceased with Jesus.

If he had been an ordinary man he would have needed many instruments and medicines, whereas Jesus had nothing but his faith. Also he would have taught others to do this healing so that it could continue after his death. Although he taught people to have faith he couldn't teach their faith to be strong enough to perform miracles.

No doubt many of those who have expressed such views would also accept an orthodox belief in Jesus as the Son of God. They have not, however, made this belief explicit. And many seem content to think of Jesus as a man with special powers—an inspired person rather than the Incarnate Son.

Of course Jesus was an ordinary man, but a special one. They say he was God's Son, but we are all God's children.

I think he was just an ordinary man, but could heal people through the Holy Spirit.

I think Jesus Christ is just like ourselves, it is just that he had powers that we do not have.

I think he had a queer power which I cannot explain.

One explicitly denies that Jesus was God's Son.

> I think he was more than an ordinary man, sent by God, but not his son. God gave him special powers to see how the people on earth would react.

Another has adoptionist views.

> My opinion is that Jesus was sent into the world as an ordinary baby, but as he grew older God gave him power to do things.

A similar opinion is put thus:

> I think of Jesus Christ as just a person chosen by God to do and show his work . . . He was in my opinion just chosen from many, but I think that he was much cleverer than us.

Others regard him variously as the Messiah, a prophet, a very religious man, or a man of the future who has gone back in time by a time machine.

Some direct attention to his goodness rather than to the miracles.

> I don't think Jesus was just an ordinary man, He seemed different from other people. He was so good, kind and gentle. You don't find people like that now.

> He was not just a clever man, he was good, kind and a great man.

But some find his goodness as great a problem as the miracles.

> You never read in the bible about him doing anything wrong. Therefore he is too good to be true.

Much effort is put into explaining how this 'ordinary' man gave the impression of being something different. He had 'talents which he put into practice'; 'he must have been a clever man'; or he had such skill that he created belief in himself:

> He could have been one of the very clever elusionists who make you believe things.

Frequent suggestions are made that the gospel narratives may be false:

> Many of the stories we read in the Bible are highly exaggerated.

And some argue that what he did then would no longer be regarded as miraculous.

> There is a lot of explanation of the things he is supposed to have done.

Things they call miracles are happening every day now, like leppers being helped or cured.

One ingenious theory attributes it all to 'good luck':

Perhaps he was a kind of doctor and all the miracles performed to people were just coincidences. He happened to visit the person when they were recovering and he received all the praise.

We are left with the handful of thorough-going sceptics.

He only made blind people see again or made lame people walk again in the words of the bible, and this could have been made up a long time ago.

If what people say about Jesus in the Bible are true, Jesus carn't have been an ordinary man. But I wouldn't take someone else's word for it.

Jesus could have been an ordinary man, or he could have been a legend created by someone for children nearly two thousand years ago.

I don't think Jesus ever existed his life is to much like a fairy tale.

I think that Jesus Christ never existed and that he was thought up by the Jewish priests to explain why so many people were not coming to the Temple.

We are left with the impression that some form of belief in God is widely accepted, and that there is widespread admiration and respect for the person of Jesus Christ. How far such attitudes are effective in determining conduct and moulding character is another question. In reading much of what the children have written one finds it all too easy to conclude that for many God and Jesus seem too remote from the contemporary world to have much influence upon everyday life. In the words already quoted:

I don't think many people think about him at all.

5 · *Is Christianity Worth Dying For?*

Well, what good would I be shot? I mean, I couldn't do much good in the world shot, so I might as well carry on living.
I don't know what good Jesus did dying on the Cross.

There are two critical questions to be asked of any system of values: Are they worth dying for? And are they worth living by? Neither of them can be genuinely answered on paper, for the first can be answered only at the stake, the second only in the strains and temptations of daily life. But the kind of answer people give to these questions reveals the measure of their insight, and if it is given as honestly as may be, though the stake is at a comfortable distance, it will reveal the kind of commitment people would at least wish to achieve.

The first question was deliberately put in the words of those who would reject the ultimate claims of Christian values on the common sense ground that though they might be good in themselves, they should not be pushed to extremes.

The largest single group accepted without hesitation the need for the ultimate sacrifice, taking up the orthodox Christian position, though sometimes on unorthodox grounds. There followed another group, about half the size of the first, who saw that a committed Christian would be ready to be killed for his faith, but who either shrank from or saw no demand for being involved themselves. Another group, little smaller than the first, rejected the call to sacrifice on either utilitarian or agnostic grounds. A final group, less than a tenth of the whole, failed to see the issue. If we divided the answers in terms of insight into the problem, we should say that the answers were equally divided: half saw that Christianity involves supreme values while the other half looked on it as at best uplift of less importance than the claims of life itself. If we divided the answers in terms of personal commitment, we should find nearly two fifths 'for' and three fifths 'against' the Christian claim.

But let us see what they say, taking first the orthodox statements.

I think that if one beleives wholly in a thing, it is worth sacrificing something for it, even if it means a life. If one is beleiving in one certain religion and just because someone thinks different, they change their mind and believe in something else, well, the strong beleif is not there, and therefore it is doing not a scrap of good. Jesus showed by dying on the Cross exactly what I am trying to point out above.

It is a good thing to dying for your religon.

Anything you realy beleve in is worth dying for.

Several were aware of the power of sacrifice to work on the hearts of other men.

If people like St Peter or St Paul had not died for their beliefs we would not have thought Christianity was worth much. If you died rather than deny your faith you would be apt to convert someone to it. Jesus died on a cross because people killed Him. He was so good the Scribes and Pharisees became afraid of His influencing the people. He was unjustly killed and when we think of Him hanging there in all His goodness it makes us realize how sinful we really are.

If you were shot because you were a christian, you wouldnt be much good dead, but other people would think more about Christianity and maybe change their Religon to Christianity it was worth dying for.

I think Jesus did a lot of good dying on the cross. He made people think.

Jesus died on the cross to save us that is what everybody believes in. I think when Jesus died everybody felt guilty about it.

By dying for Christianity it makes people think why the person did so. The Suffregettes tied themselves to railings to create attention. By dying on a cross Jesus created attention and showed that he was willing to die for his beliefs.

Some answers draw the analogy with patriotism.

You might say the last war wasn't worth fighting about. But men were only fighting for their beliefs.

If men have to die for there country then if necessary, their religion is also worth dying for.

Others perceive the obstinacy of conscience ('If you gave in you would have it on your conchons all your life'), or of love for persons ('If you love a person moor than any one or anything you would be willing to give your life for him'). Some betray an improbable stoicism ('If your are a good Christian you must take what comes to you and choose the right or wrong way with a cheerful smile as Jesus did'). And some (though curiously few) touch on the hope of eternal reward so strong in medieval Christianity, and so often assumed by agnostics to be the prime Christian motive.

If you do die for Christianity you may get some benefit from it from the place where you go when you leave this earth. Many people on this earth would remember why and what you did it for.

Finally, there creeps in the belief in re-incarnation, here curiously blended with orthodoxy.

Yes! Christianity is worth dying for. God thought we were worth giving up his son for so surely we can give up our life for God. Another thin is that I believe in reincarnation and therefore when you die you will be born again as a new person.

The next group contains those who can see that Christian belief might make its ultimate claims on the committed, but feel no sense of commitment themselves.

If you realy beleave in God and Christianity you wouldn't mine being shot because you no where your going and you have died gracefully.

I dont think so, but people who beleave in him would.

Some people believe in Jesus so much that they would give their life for him but others wouldn't because they dont believe in him. I dont quite know whether I do or not.

A true Christian will think that Christianity is worth dying for, but I am not *yet* a true Christian I would not die.

I personally would not have the courage to dye for Christianity.

I dont think anything is worth dying for unless you have a great fath in it.

One or two were irritated by the folly of the proposition ('I think it's stupid to give your life up for something you dont care much about. I like the life I'm living now'). And one was suspicious of hypocrisy and heroics ('Some of the people who say they are willing to be shot because of thier religion are just trying to make themselves into HEROES').

Among the utilitarians are many, as we should expect, who do little more than echo the quotation.

I dont think Christianity is worth dying for.

If a man were to die for Christianity today it would be in the papers one day, and forgotten the next.

No i don't think Christianity is worth dying for what good as it done us.

Matrys did not do much good by geting burnt did they?

Some speak from the instinct to survival, so strong with the young. A few are prepared to concede the value of martyrdom for an old person ('about seventy') who has done all the good he can. Others simply shrink from the thought for themselves.

I would take up any religion to stay alive.

I don't want to die and I wouldn't know what I was dying for anyway.

I think it is worth living you must enjoy yourself when you are young because you are only young once.

Many try to come to grips with the problem, and weigh up one good against another, emphasizing the doubtful value of witness in death against the claims of service, preaching (even 'teaching scripture to younger people') or care for a family.

I believe with this because if you were dead you couldn't go around helping people because you would be dead.

You conn't teach people about God from your grave.

You are more helpful when you are alive especially if you have a family to take care of.

Some look on religion as a private affair, with no significant public responsibility.

I agree with this, if you keep on living you can carry out the work you began, in secret. And as for dying for what you think, no one can take thoughts and knowledge away from you.

I would go on living because you can still be a christian inside.

Others try to make a historical judgement on the achievement of Christianity.

There is just as much suffering and hardship in the world as there was years ago, with refugees and people like that.

Jesus didnt do any good for mankind when he killed himself because people still murder and rob today.

Yet another attempt at historical assessment comes from those who argue that the present state of civilization renders the question academic.

It might have been a long time ago when people had only just heard about Christ, and the people died because others would not let them preach the word of God. But nowadays everyone preaches what he believes and no one stops them. So why die.

The same line of thought appears in the less controversial form of a value-judgement.

I think that people should be allowed to lead their own life and there should be no reason for dying just because somebody else believes different kinds of things to you, and I do not think Jesus should have had such a painfull death.

Finally, in this group come the agnostics and sceptics who reject the claim to sacrifice because they are either doubtful of the truth of Christianity or certain of its untruth.

We dont know if Jesus dying on the Cross made any difference to our life today and I dont suppose we ever will.

They say the church grew bigger when Jesus was crucified, but how do we know, we wasn't there. If it was proved to me that there was a God, and he was a good man, I might die for him, but while nothing has been proved to me that there is a God, I think I would rather live and have my thoughts.

No because it it just a religion resulting from a fabrication of the Jewish priests.

We dont even know if he did, it is only what we have been told to believe.

From the last group, a few random quotations will illustrate the sort of confusion that arises, ranging from muddled orthodoxy to muddled unorthodoxy, and including those who confess to being puzzled.

Jesus was right dieing on the cross it showed us what wicked people the human race was at that time.

I know Jesus died on the cross but I don't really see how by doing this he saved us.

Jesus could have prevented himself from dying if he was as good as they make him out to be.

Jesus died on the cross for a reason. The reason was to fulfil the phrophesies.

I don't know properly what he was trying to prove but whatever it was it would have to be a good reason for a man to give his life.

I dont think Christianity is worth dying for. It would probably give you a good second life so you might as well finish you first one and enjoy it.

I just cant see any advantage in dying for Christianity. Because those who go to heaven if there is one must be good to get there so whats the use of dying unless your bad.

If you kill a person you have to take what you are given. If you are shot it must be for a good reason unless you are shot by a murderer.

6 · *Is it Boring to be Good?*

On the whole, do you prefer to be *made* to be good, or do you prefer to be allowed to be bad if you want?
I'd rather be bad.
And are you prepared to take the consequences of being bad?
Yes.
Well, it would be ever so dull with everybody being good and cheerful and so on. It changes the routine if somebody is bad once in a while.
You have to be a bit cheeky to get on, anyway.

The interest in this exchange lies in its stinging tail. On the general issue of compulsion and freedom there would be little argument: the right to err is implicit in our culture, and only the neurotically insecure would fail to claim it, and be prepared for its consequences. Most of us, however, would prefer to formulate the doctrine with a bias towards goodness, demanding choice but hoping for the right choice. Here, on the contrary, being 'bad, once in a while' is made to appear desirable in itself: goodness is dull, and badness makes a change, while 'cheekiness' is indispensable in the struggle to get on.

Before we begin to suspect our adolescents of a positive will to evil, we must remember that 'being made to be good' means the continuation of the school situation with its prohibitions and its fussy rules, its monotony and predictability, while 'being allowed to be bad' means achieving the status of an adult. Furthermore, 'badness' is not evil. To the child, badness is naughtiness, with its spicing of fun and adventure, conducted within the school or home situation in which the consequences will be controlled. A little fun is worth paying for, they argue; but they are not aware—how could they be aware?—of the fearful price that might have to be paid.

There are thus no more than half a dozen children to favour being made to be good, as this one does:

> One should be made to be good and the ones being bad should take a punishment. If everyone was good life would be cheerful and everyone would be much happier.

Many more than these few, however, are in favour of goodness in principle while accepting the necessity of a free choice of evil.

> I'd rather be bad if I wanted to.

> I would rather be given the chose of being bad.

> I would much rather like to behave and be good myself than to have somone to make me good. Although at times I get into bad moods.

The justification of goodness springs from many motives: altruism ('I'd rather be good because, when your good you don't go against anyone'); making the world a better place ('there would be no wars or fighting and everything would be peaceful'); getting on with people; getting on ('people will get a good apinegne of you and you will get on in life'); and the converse, in the imprudence of being bad ('Look at all these teddy boys who round breaking into shops and stealing and it does not get them anywhere'). Here is an answer that gathers together many of the points:

> No I dont want to be *made* to be good. God gave me a free will so that I can choose between wrong and right. Life would be terrible if there was no freedom of choice. If you are bad you often make life awful for other people. If I am bad (which is often) I am willing to take the consequences. Life is much nicer when people are good and cheerful and so on. I do not agree that it is boring, it makes you feel 'good' deep down inside.

This last point, that 'goodness' is rewarding, and not merely boring, is often made:

> When you have done something good such as guiding blind people home and doing other good things you feel very pleased with yourself inside.

> People benifit from your cheerfulness and goodness, and you get happiness from that.

It worries you for a long time afterwards when you have done something bad.

It is not boring to be happy. If everyone was happy the world would go on much better, with no fights, no quarrels, and no argueing.

If you are unhappy yourself and you make others who you come into contact with unhappy too, especially your parents.

The greatest insight into the situation is shown by the substantial group who make an attempt to draw the line between harmless naughtiness and genuine evil.

Well I dont think it hurts anyone to do something wrong once in a while as long as it isn't really bad. I find it fun to do something wrong somtimes, but I wouldn't call it bad. I mean if your at the pictures for example and you sing with the picture and your told not to and you still do it isn't bad it's just a bit of fun. If I do something I like to get on with it instead of people saying oh isn't she good our so an' so wouldn't do that it really makes me sick especiall if I'm the so an so. I like to do things off of my own back.

To this extent, most of our children agree with the quotation. One favours 'a little flutter of badness', another thinks it is 'best to be just in between'. 'There is being good and being good', observes one child sagely.

It is nice to be bad accaisionally, but only doing little things and not things like bullying or stealing.

This mild badness may be a prophylactic against worse:

If youre good youre just little innecent all the time you are going get bored and more likely if you don't do something wrong one day youre going to do something that is very wrong and you have got to let youre self go once in a while.

A certain indulgence, indeed, may contribute to the happiness of others.

If a person is too good and angelic it can be very boring for them and for everybody around them.

And even 'being cheeky' can be subjected to analysis.

There is no need to be delibratty cheecky to somebody older than yourself because this is usualy just being rude. You should stand up for yourselve not let people walk over you. But there is difference between not letting people walk over you and being cheeky.

A youngster with an epigrammatic gift sums up this general attitude:

A little bit of bad, with twice as much good, makes a man human.

It is the desire to be 'human' that moves the majority of those who speak up in favour of badness.

I would rather be bad than a goody goody.

Some fear the weight of a good reputation ('Boys will think you a snob'); others fear monotony ('If every person was identical what a terrible world this would be')—even the monotony of badness:

It is boring to be too good but it must also be boring to be too bad. So its best to be just in between.

I enjoy being good when I am, but that is not very often. Because I have more fun when I'm bad. I wouldn't rather be bad all the time but most of the time.

One child carries this horror of monotony into his speculation about the after-life:

That has always worried me about heaven every thing run so smovely nobody ever does any thing. I should be terribly bored.

The evil deeds that these children contemplate are rarely specified, and when they are, they are of the order of the singing at the pictures already described; how dull, they argue, to keep quiet when the teacher is out of the room, always to be polite, and to give way to others' whims!

It would be agreed that there is little harm in all this. The general response is sane and healthy, but immature and heavily marked by a childish view of goodness. 'Be good', they have heard, day in day out, for years: and 'Be good' has meant 'Be quiet; do what you are told; don't do what you have not been told; beware of originality; follow the beaten track; above all, don't cause me any trouble.' The vision of a world in which everyone is busy toeing lines is as unattractive to the young as it is to the rest of us, and, even at some cost, they would like the picture made less tidy. At the same time there is an abundance of moral responsibility, the readiness to scrutinize a situation for its importance and an act for the degree of its power to hurt. And there is a good will towards goodness, an understanding of the moral ideal. What is lacking is inevitably experience; less inevitably, some of the tools of moral dialectic; and, most deplorably, any suggestion of the Christian content of 'goodness', with its adventurousness, its creativeness, its transcendence of the rules.

7 · *Life after Death*

I'd say there's a heaven if you believe in Jesus, but there's a heaven because you think you're going to Jesus, but if you've never believed in Jesus, then you don't know where you're going.

Well, I don't think there's a place like heaven. I think that you kind of come back into the world again, to live and lead a better life, and you go on coming back until you're perfect, and then, well there isn't a place, but I think you go to God when you're perfect. When you're fit to go to him.

To ask boys and girls of fourteen to expound the doctrine of eternal life is obviously to ask too much. But an interest in it is characteristic of adolescence, and our young people have tackled the problem with zest. This is as it should be, for the problem of death is merely the other side of the medal to the problem of life. Adolescents are being challenged to find meaning in life; and one of the questions they must be expected to ask is, Well, then, what meaning does it have when it is over?

At first sight the choice seems fairly simple: to 'believe' or 'disbelieve' in a life after death. We may settle, with the early Hebrews, for what it looks like: 'Man is like to vanity: his days are as a shadow that passeth away.' Or we may protest that there must be more to it than this. Scepticism is here so easy, so obvious, that we chose our quotations with a bias towards belief. The first remark comes from a pious evangelical, the second from the curious streak of re-incarnationism, respectable in the east, odd, yet morally attractive, in the west. With these two views before them, it was hoped that the rationalists would have no difficulty in dismissing the entire concept; while the accepting orthodox and the thinking, serious-minded doubters, would have some provocation to comment.

And this was what happened. The believers constituted more than half of the group, and wrote with high confidence. Some of them follow the first speaker in making use of Christian imagery, and regarding survival as in some way a direct result of belief in Christ.

> I think there is a heaven. Jesus said there was. If there isn't, then where do our souls go when we die?

> I think there is a heaven, but you won't go there if you do not believe in Jesus Christ.

> I believe there is a heaven. I don't think you stop in your grave for the rest of your life, and I don't think you come back to this earth but you have to go somewhere and I think heaven is where you go.

A few have settled down to a forbidding, a rather frightening, certainty:

> I believe in Jesus Christ so *I know* that I am going to heaven. As for the people who don't believe in Jesus Christ, I can also answer that. They will be going to hell.

Happily, there are rather more to take a hopeful view, either by rejecting hell altogether:

> I believe there is a heaven but not a hell;

or by admitting to heaven a wider range of desert:

> I think there is a heaven, and I think God takes good and bad.

In one or two instances, the doctrine of purgatory appears:

> I think that if you are bad you will be cured in heaven.

Speculation about what goes on in heaven is specifically excluded by Christian teaching, but it is natural and not improper to endeavour to give some content to the idea. One child has a fairly clear picture:

> I think there is such a place as heaven. I believe that heaven is a far away planet which has not been discovered. When you die, if your accepted for going to heaven, your soul is taken to this planet and you meet there all your relations and friends whom you lost in your mortal life. In heaven, everything is perfect and your soul lives on and never dies. I believe that the souls of dead people can watch over their friends on earth and sort of talk to them in their minds.

Others are less specific, but try to convey the notion of eternal bliss, and compensation for the trials of earthly life:

I think that there is a new world where everyone's happy and you always live there and meet everybody there again.

I believe that there is another world. I dont know where, better and cleaner than our world. We are put on this earth to test us.

A few are suspicious of the prospect of endless bliss:

I think there is a place where you go after you have died, but I dont think it will be so wonderful as it is sometimes made out to be.

So much for the large number who, even with their minor reservations, seem content to accept the idea of heaven as at least an emotional necessity. In contrast, there is a smaller, but still significant group, who can do without it. Some are simply not interested.

I do not think there is a heaven. I think we are just buried and that is where we stay.

I don't believe there is such a place as heaven. When your dead you're dead. Some people preach there is a place called heaven— others say it is on earth—I don't care where it is.

Some, realizing that the existence of the belief may need some explanation, seek to rationalize it as a fictitious moral incentive.

I don't think there is a heaven because you all gets buried in the same sort of place. How on earth can you get out of a coffin and six feet of dirt and take a trip to the sky. I think it is just another thing to make you good.

I'd say heaven is just a fantasy to give people peace of mind when they die.

Others are preoccupied by the problem of geography, the incomprehensibility of heaven as a 'place', its size and its location.

I dont think there is a heaven because if there was it would have to be a pretty big place to take all the good people who have died.

I wouldn't say there's a heaven—nobody's ever spoken to any one who says they've been. All we can see is a mass of clouds.

It is no doubt this physical difficulty that leads one child to write, flatly:

There could be a heaven, but science has proved this wrong.

When we have extracted these two, fairly confident groups, we are left with a more subtle division between those who would like to accept the idea of heaven, but are aware of its difficulties, and those who reject it, but are not prepared to assert the complete corollary, that life is self-contained, and has no meaning beyond.

These last take up the suggestion of re-incarnation offered by the second speaker in our quotation:

> I'm not struck on saying there is a heaven. I think you come back to life again.

> I think when I die I will come back as someone else and carry on like that. I don't believe in heaven and hell because millions of people are dying every day, and there wouldn't be enough room for us all, we would be meeting stone age men and so on.

> I don't believe in heaven. I think people just die and are born again (re-incarnated).

> I don't think there is a heaven. Nobody's been there and come back so nobody knows. When you die you come into the world as someone else.

Some believe that this approach has scientific support:

> There is no proof that there is a heaven—it is a belief of people who think when they die their souls and minds go there. Scientists today are experimenting on people who can tell of their experiences of a few hundred years ago. In other words, they have either come back to earth or not left it. I will only believe there is a heaven if the people in the expriments talk about having been there or when I go there myself.

From the other, more orthodox side, comes an effort to convey the notion of another order of existence, inconceivable to our space-bound minds, but recognizable in terms of value.

> Heaven is not like a city or such but something abstract like happiness, its something which you look forward to when you die somewhere where worry strain or heartbreak etc. doesnt exist. I think heaven is not a place above the clouded that's for children to belive in. I belive heaven his in the person. Heaven is like God you cannot see it or tuch it but it is there.

> I think that heaven is in the heart, not in the clouds or any other place because that is where the goodness will come from.

> Oh! I believe that heaven is all around you, and not way up in the clouds. I also believe that it is part of the mind.

I also feel that if you believe, there is a heaven. Not as we used to think of it as up in the sky, but as place for God in your hearts.

Heaven is where God is and he is all around us.

Finally, we have a handful people who have no confidence either that we know anything or that the problem is worth thinking about.

how Do I now theres a heaven or you I Dot think there a heaven.

To the above question I honestly have not got an answer to it.

realy none of us nos where we will go.

Nobody nose.

There emerges from these quotations a picture of minds at work on the problem. In the nature of things, we should not expect them to have made much progress; and the interest shown, and the wide realization that any position has its difficulties, may be regarded as encouraging.

At the same time, it is plain that many of the children are handicapped by a literalism of interpretation which prevents insight into the real issue. The Christian who is satisfied with the concept of heaven as a 'place' to be reached in the distant future may find a simple solution to the problem of evil and an equally simple incentive for the moral struggle, but he is unlikely to enter the new dimension presented by the full Christian doctrine of eternity. And the rationalist who dismisses the whole notion as impossible, inconceivable, merely because it does not fit into the normal categories of proof, turns his back on the immediate spiritual issues of life.

8 · *The Problem of Suffering*

Is it fair of God to allow suffering?

God couldn't care for us or else he would stop all accidents, murders and things like that.

When we trailed this remark before our children, we hoped it might provoke some of them to take the first step in dealing with the problem, which is to discriminate between different kinds of suffering. Much suffering springs from a direct offence against the laws of nature, and we cannot protest against it without protesting against the idea of law. Much springs from involuntary ignorance of the laws of nature, and while ignorance offers an 'excuse' for the offence, and arouses our pity for the offender, we can rationally accept the consequent suffering as part of the seriousness of life. If we never suffered from the consequences of ignorance and folly, there would be no point in knowledge and wisdom. A vast amount of suffering springs from the failure of our highest hopes: the vision of what might be convinces us that it ought to be, and we are bitterly disappointed when it is not.

Something of this discrimination is implicit in the quotation. There is clearly a difference between accidents and murders. There is the provocation of the word 'fair,' a cultural rather than a natural concept. And only when these two items have been clarified can we come to grips with the work of God, and the proposition that he does or does not 'care'; and behind this, the doctrine of the omnipotence of God.

A few traces of an attempt to make this analysis may be found, but for the most part our children accepted the word 'suffering' as a package, conceived of God as a manager of the universe able to arrange its details as he pleases, and proceeded rather desperately to look for some way out of the obvious difficulty.

Only a very few were here content with pious words, the uncritical assertion that all is for the best.

God has got a reason for everything He does.

I don't believe that God is cruel and would make us suffer without reason.

These children have given up the problem presented by the facts.

The rationalists, as we should expect, have given up the other end of the problem, the omnipotence and nature of God. A few are sure that God does not exist:

If there was a God He would stop all pain and accidents.

Others imply that even if he does exist he cannot care:

God does not care.

> I think He should stop some of the terrible things what happen if He really cares.

> God daft.

Neither of these positions can be said to be constructive. The Christian who wraps himself in his faith in the beneficent ordering of things turns his back on the realities of the human situation; and the rationalist who sees no problem loses all motive to find an explanation.

But most of our children do seek for an explanation. Many of them, stern little school-moralists as they are, are attracted by the use of suffering as punishment.

> I think when God allows suffering that it is punishment for something they have done in the past.

> God must have a reason for letting us suffering, if we do not suffer some time in our lives any could happen. Because people suffer for doing wrong.

> God let people who murder suffer in the end.

> I teaches us to be more carfull in the feuture.

There is something of the school situation in all this: suffering takes its part in the system of incentives, and may be expected to fill the same rôle in the real world. One writer said that it was not necessary to 'know what you'd done: you just take the punishment, headache or polio, in faith'. Suffering thus becomes God's instrument of education, the only way he has of 'getting anywhere with us'. We may run the risk attached to breaking rules as we do for diversion in school life; but God will catch up with us, as teacher will.

Even the examination offers some analogy:

> It is probable one of his ways of testing us murder or crimes or such like are very hard to understand but it is believ that everything has some reason behind it.

Some go beyond the mechanical notion of legal punishment, and approach that of character-building. Suffering makes men tougher mentally and physically for it gives them something to compete with. It is the stuff that heroes are made of. God allows it to see just how much we can stand: or to stop us taking things for granted, feeling too secure or too much at home on earth, or getting ideas above our station.

If God kept us free from accidents we would take it for granted that we were something special and start corrupting the world.

A grimmer note is struck by those who see suffering as a means of population control (and here, surely, a little elementary analysis of kinds of suffering might have been undertaken).

If God didn't allow some suffering there would be even more over-crowding in the world than there is now.

You have got to have a certain amount of suffering or the world would be over run by humans and animals.

Nobody saw that this is merely a contradiction in terms, and that it is death, not suffering, that reduces the population; but there were several who clutched at this way out while dimly aware that it is unsatisfactory.

If God does not allow suffering then the world would be over-crowded. But it does seem terrible that many hundreds of people die every week. I never realized it until a few weeks ago, and it has never happened to my family.

And the same note of rebellious pity appears in a use of the punishment theme:

I think God do care for us; and just allowed things like this to go on so as to punish us, but I wish there was a better way to do this.

The same, Job-like, Blakeian protest occurs repeatedly, reflecting the new awareness of the horror of much of life that presents so acute a challenge to the adolescent, as he moves out of his well-ordered, domestic system.

When a young baby dies I cant believe it's god's doing or will. Like in World War II the terrible suffering under the rule of the Nazis. I still cant believe it was God's will for 12 million innocent people to die in the gas chambers.

A few have heard, but without comprehending, that the suffering of Christ throws light on the problem.

God's son suffered. We are His sons and daughters so we must suffer.

One or two go a little further, and see that the Cross is in some way connected with the freedom of the human race.

When God gave us life he meant us to accept all responsibilities. Pain, grief and sadness. After all Jesus suffered on the Cross terrible pain.

If God did has this statment would like humans would not have to freedom to disied there own destination in life.

The appeal to freedom ranges from an intentional, 'created' freedom, as in

God makes the people only and he doesn't make them do everything they lead their own lives and made to fend for themselves

to the picture of a beneficent, well-intentioned deity who has set the whole process in motion, but in the face of man's wrong-headedness, stands by almost helpless. He started something and has now lost control over it.

I don't think God allows suffering; He just hasn't the power to stop it.

Jesus when on earth did what He could by healing but God can't do much now.

Some take refuge in regarding God as in some way withdrawn from parts of the universe:

God can't be in each particular place at once,

while others frankly accept the devil:

God has no hand over wicked people; the devil rules them.

God has nothing to do with this wicked world, it is the devil's.

Others attribute suffering to the human will, and make use of the Genesis story to illustrate it. Eve's disobedience over the 'two trees' led to all this suffering in childbirth and toil in the fields and to Cain's murder of his brother, for God gave everyone 'a sense of will-power', and we must dominate each other. And so we fight wars, and this will always be until God destroys the human race or lets it destroy itself.

Nearly all these comments may be grouped under three general attitudes: simple trust, simple protest, or puzzled, and largely unsatisfactory attempts at an 'explanation'. We may conclude with one, far from typical, example from a child who sees that the search for explanation is here less important than the development of a creative and constructive attitude:

God loves us and does not want us to suffer. That is why there are doctors and nurses to treat accidents and illness. Many have become better people through suffering, their character have been strengthened. God sent His Son to die that, when men die, they might know no more suffering.

9 · *Is Prayer Any Use?*

I like it when we pray for the sick. I think that something really happens when you pray for sick people and the old.

This simple, rather touching statement offers a clear line of division between believers and unbelievers; and proposes for the believers several points for discussion: the effect of prayer on the person praying ('I like it'); its effect on the person prayed for ('something really happens); its general usefulness, and its specific uses ('sick people and the old').

The believers were in the over-whelming majority; and the tone of four fifths of the comments would support the claim that 'man is a praying animal'. Repeatedly we are given the impression that here is something primal, a spontaneous activity carrying comfort and reassurance to which man turns in his need, perhaps especially when he is intellectually perplexed.

I like praying I think most of our prayers are answered and I pray regular and most of my prayers have come true.

Yes I think prayer is of some use to us because it gives you confidence in God.

I like to pray for old people and the sick.

I always pray every night. It comforts me to speak to God and ask for help and forgiveness. When I am in trouble I always turn to God and although I don't realise, when I think of it it always turns out better.

Most were confident that God answers prayer, though from some came a recognition that we must not trust to it as a magic formula for getting our own way: we should always say 'Thy will be done' and not try to force God's hand.

I agree with praying for the sick but when you pray for something you want you feel that they are sometimes ignored and sometimes notice is taken of them.

This warning takes sometimes the positive form that 'you must pray properly'. One child defined this as 'keeping on at it': and the parable of the importunate widow had obviously had its effect in emphasizing faith and persistence. You must not only pray when in trouble. If you want to be heard in time of crisis, you must have worn your path to the throne by regular normal prayer. 'Properly' may also be taken to mean 'confined to reasonable requests'. After all, one child observes, God has his limits. And 'reasonable requests' may be defined as 'spiritual' rather than material benefit.

God only gives comfort to mind and growth and does not give man-made products.

Most children, indeed, were prepared to leave aside the difficult problem of an actual 'answer' to prayer, in the sense of an occurrence or an act of God, while firmly convinced of its value to the person praying.

I like praying because it gives some sort of ease to me.

If you pray it makes you feel there is some hope for what you are praying for.

Prayer is of use. I usually get terribly worried and frightened about my exams, but last time I took them I started to pray to God weeks before they started, and when they came I was telling all my friends not to worry! Prayer can also help the sick, sorrowing or worried.

Even if your prayers aren't answered, I think that to pray brings peace of mind.

Even in praying for the sick, part of the value may lie in the new confidence that comes to the one praying: you feel you have done something; 'it gives you a sense of power to heal'.

In my opinion prayer is very useful because you feel as though you've helped someone without them knowing but to want many things is not a pray and will be of little use to anyone.

One long answer is worth quoting for a number of reasons:

Prayer is most essential. The C. of E. prayers I couldn't imagine getting very far but a prayer from the heart goes further. Two years ago we tried for a site for a new church. The council said we couldn't have it but through prayer we got it. Then people said it was impossible to get the money but people sent in gifts from as far off as Lancashire who we'd never heard of. One gentleman decided to sell up his business and give the money. We borrowed some and now, in a few weeks, the church on the estate will start to go up.

This need for 'prayer from the heart' is often mentioned, and is probably conceived in terms of the contrast between liturgical and extempore prayer.

Most of us feel prayer is a good thing when it has a meaning. But when you mumble the same thing day after day it loses all meaning and is a wast of time.

In all this there is little awareness of the varied elements in prayer, though one or two suggest that there is more to prayer than asking, even for the sick and aged:

Prayers are for thanking or asking.

When you pray for the sick and for old people you ask God a favour. But do you ever thank God for the things He has given you? You should, you know.

But none of this amounts to a view of prayer as a relationship with God, or an integral part of a whole way of life. It remains an almost instinctive activity, performed in certain moods and for certain ends; but always intermittent, deliberate, ultimately utilitarian.

It is against this view of prayer that the rationalists react in the way we should expect them to. Some are wistful and regretful that they are unconvinced.

Although I like praying does it really help or is it the doctor?

God can see our needs without prayers.

Prayer is not satisfying to God. He prefers action.

Who can tell if it is of any use?

Others are more cheerfully convinced that it is pointless.

Really I think that it is the patient that gets better on his own, and that God does not help.

I cannot see wot praying can do for the sick. You can not make them better by talking or praying.

Just a wast of time Prayer.

Take life as it comes, it turns out all right. It's often just luck.

And one confident materialist dismissed the matter with:

I've never tried it.

This attitude is curiously rarer in the discussion on prayer than on more remote themes, such as the nature of God or the divinity of Christ. Even the rationalist recognizes the widespread appeal of prayer and seeks to explain it.

It's a human weakness tha we must have someone to lean on so we pray.

We are left with the impression that here is a problem that matters. The adolescent is still a child in being powerfully moved by what he can do, and apprehensive and uncertain about what he can only know or believe: indeed, do not most of us in this respect remain children to the end? Most of our children agree that when we have prayed we feel we have done something; and few of them are ready to abandon this hope of 'doing something', however deeply they feel the difficulties of its theory. We may have here a clue to an approach to religious education that may illumine the whole shadowy and uncertain field.

10 · *Going to Church*

Every church has the same atmosphere—a dead atmosphere.

I don't like going to church because there aren't any people of my own age there. I don't think I'd be welcome.

The schools are compelled to be neutral in all matters that might stir up denominational rivalry; and since we cannot go to church without going to a denomination, we should not expect church-going to be discussed except in the most general terms. But we asked our children to comment on it, because the scripture teacher cannot define his task unless he knows what help his children may count on from their church life. Religious instruction may be defended as a mere school subject (as part of a liberal education, as a foundation course in moral philosophy, as moral training, as a part of cultural history, as a dimension of the human imagination) but its content, method, and expectation of success—its ultimate intention—must be radically affected by the extent to which the church plays its part in the creation of fellowship, the engagement of the will and the deepening of the spirit of worship.

We thus asked our children to align themselves 'for' or 'against' the church, suggesting two lines of discussion: Do you like church when you get there? And do you feel that the church likes you?

The answers divide fairly evenly between those who approve and those who disapprove. Some children speak from a happy experience of church going. Well, they say, I like it.

I like the church as it seems more reverent.

I like going to church because it has a peaceful and calmness about it.

Some go further than this, and take their critics to task, roundly urging them to approach their church-going in a proper spirit.

Of course you're welcome in the Church. You just don't give yourself a chance to know the church better.

Everybody is welcome in our Church. If you don't feel welcome, have a word with the Vicar or the Priest.

Not every church is the same if you want to go to a merry church and where there is young people you cannot just go to one church and judge the rest of the churches by it.

Most church clubs encourage their members to attend church services. It does not matter if no body of your own age is there you are not going to have to dance with them! You are there to worship God. Take some of your friends who are the same. In a local church magazine the church was arguing that all new members were to be welcomed by the other members of the church if they were young or old.

Many argue that church is not meant to be jolly; it is meant for serious devotion.

Whether you are the youngest or the oldest in church it should not worry you People go to church to pray and sing, not to see who is the youngest or the oldest.

Of course church is dead, and is not the place for having a good time with your friends. Church is meant for praying to God, and to go to when in trouble or lonely. You do not expect it to have parties &c.

Granted every church as the same atmosphere but it is not a 'dead' atmosphere'. It is an atmosphere which I think cannot be really explained except by yourself, it is what you yourself feel when you enter a church and the silence.

There are surely some people of one's own age there, if not why not try to get friends to go to Church. And as for not being welcome is just not true as to what ever church you enter as a Christian you are always welcome.

A considerable number, still clearly speaking from personal experience, are more critical.

The Vicar is too dreary. They talk of things children couldn't understand and I don't like church. I would rather play out.

All, or most churches have a dead atmosphere, in my opinion. It's just a matter of going sitting and listening. You get no chance to discuss.

Every church has a dull mourning sort of atmosphere. The services are to long and usually the sermon is very dull. I think that prayers at home are just as good, maybe I've convinced myself of this as an excuse not to go to church and be bored.

I hate going to church, I think its boring sitting there for hours on end as it seems, listening to the priest blabering on and on. It isn't the same in all churches though, the Salvation Army is one I like.

Some think that church services could be made more lively, no doubt inspired by press reports of 'teen-age' services.

I think that if church was a bit more livelier a lot more teenagers would go. Say to jazz the songs and prayers up.

But this suggestion is rejected by one earnest soul:

... if they painted them bright colours and jazzed up the hymns they would only listen to the music and not take in what was trying to be taught them and the Lord's house would not be His any more.

For the rest, the criticisms of the church are such as we might hear in any street-corner conversation. Churchgoers are hypocrites:

Herpocresy because some people do it to show off when they do not believe in God.

They are merely conventional:

> The main body of the congregation nowardays goes to church be-
> cause 'it's good for you' not because they are religious.

They are opportunists with an eye on the life to come:

> You find nearly all old people going to church because I think they
> want to get on the good side of God before they die.

Or they are wasting their time:

> I don't like going to church because I don't see what good it
> does you.

Some children complain that they were forced to go too often
when they were young; others that they have enough religion at
school.

> We learn all about the bible and God in school hours I think
> Sunday should be made at home.

There is nothing in all this to cause any surprise, little that most
members of a congregation have not felt, at times, themselves.
Regular churchgoers have sometimes to struggle alone making
their own prayer 'from the heart' with, seemingly, no comfort
from without. So far we should accept much of what these
children say as a fair and not unhopeful statement. But it is a
slender hope. Even those who profess themselves friendly to the
church do not see that it is greater than their own feelings. As
they like praying because it is a comfort, so they like the church;
but they have not seen the church as the community in which
Meaning is to be found, the altar of their dedication, the promise
of their hope, the source of a life that will flow into their everyday
struggle. They could not, at fourteen, see much of this; but if they
see none of it, then they are not even on the way.

Most of them, we know from other sources, are going to drop
the habit of churchgoing when they begin to work; and then what
remains? The confusion of thought we have seen illustrated in
the previous sections cannot be sorted out alone; and the deep
concern and lively interest in the mystery of existence will
wither away.

11 · *Religious Instruction*

Well, I think as we grew older they were still telling us the same kind of things, instead of more adultish things.

There's too much thinking done for you.

Yes, it's much more interesting when you can discuss than just be taught.

So far we have been concerned with the results of religious education in terms of insight and understanding. Here we ask our commentators for their reaction to its content and method. Are they learning what they feel they need to know? And is it being presented in a way that meets their needs?

The replies were overwhelmingly in favour of more 'adultishness' in content and more discussion in class. But it is not easy to discover what is meant by 'adultishness' or what themes should be discussed. To the adolescent 'adult' is a highly coloured word, representing his hopes of status and importance, seriousness, the hope of becoming. He values his experience as it comes in adult form: his clothes, his freedom, his responsibility; and though he knows he is not really grown up, he is always conscious of being a little more grown up than older people seem to think. To ask him, therefore, as our quotation asks him, 'Would you like to study more adult things?' is to expect the answer 'Yes'.

The considerable group who answer 'No' are therefore peculiarly significant. A few of these suspect that they are not themselves sufficiently adult to cope with anything much more advanced than they have been receiving.

If you really think you will find out it is not the things you are taught are not babish but if you think like an adult your lessons will seem more grown up.

The older one gets and the more one thinks about all kinds of things to do with Christianity things that you might have heard over and over again take on a different aspect and become 'more adultish things'.

Some make the point that the lesson has to be learnt, even if it does involve some repetition.

I partly agree with this, but they were only trying to make you realise what a wonderful man God was.

Indeed some find adult themes unintelligible:

> We used to have lessons on the Bible when we were in another teacher's class, but now we have a different teacher we have gone straight on to *adult* religion and I am very puzzled sometimes I think if we were led into it gradually we would understand it better.

But these defenders of simple Bible instruction are rare. More common are those who defend the charge against their scripture teaching on the grounds that it is not true in their class. One child observed shrewdly:

> I think that manly depends on the person teaching you.

And nearly a third assert that for them an adult approach has begun, and they like it. What do they mean by 'adult' here? Some mean a new treatment of the Bible:

> I think as we grow older we are taught the theory side of the Bible such as what the things mean scientificly our teacher does anyway.

This may include the higher criticism:

> In the school I attend they have explained the Bible may not all be true, that the stories may only be based on the truth. And I think that is the way most girls and boys would like to be taught.

For others, the shift to 'adultishness' is away from the Bible to what are presumably everyday problems.

> We don't always learn about the Bible, but other things which grown ups discuss.

> I have thought that as we grow older, we would still have lessons on the Bible. But I seem to have been wrong, for the older you get the less you think of the Bible.

The clues we have as to this different subject-matter are rare: other religious books, the lives of great men, the lives of saints instead of 'out of date' people in the Bible.

Though we thus receive little guidance in the meaning of 'adultishness' from those who approve of their religious instruction, we have a flood of condemnation of childishness and repetitiveness from those who disapprove.

> Right up to our forth year at our school we are still being taught things we learnt in our very first year.

I have heard some storys over and over again with just a little orterration but they are never made more adultish as we get older.

When you first come to school when you are 5 yrs. old after a year they start to tell you about Jesus. Then after about 8 yrs. when you are at 13-14 they are still telling you the same.

When I was at the goner school they told hows the same.

Some parables and miracles are repeated time and time again in Bible lessons until we know them inside out, back to front or upside down. Take Josep and his coat of many colours this is one in particular which is very often repeated.

Lessons on the Bible are the same all yor life Verey Bul.

One criticism suggests that the use of the lectionary and the feasts of the Church has overridden the need for a progressive syllabus:

The bible is boring because it never changes its story its the same story for a different time of the year ever year.

This kind of comment comes from about half our children. The force of it is weakened a little if we remember that the quotation had suggested the line of argument 'they were still telling us the same thing'. But it must be apparent by now that the children are perfectly ready to disagree with what was said; and this warm endorsement must be taken seriously. The story of Joseph and his coat, at all events, does not call for much repetition.

At the same time, mere variety of theme and treatment does not provide the answer.

All teachers tell you different versions of the same story and you don't know who to believe.

While some things are too difficult:

Some lessons are quite interesting but then you get those that are to difficult to understand and these become boring.

And others suggest that the Bible is adult, but its treatment is not:

Well there is not much in the Bible that is childish, but I think the main trouble is the way in which its taught makes it 'unadultish'.

Finally, we may quote from the small, surprisingly small, number who seize this opportunity of saying that Bible lessons should be discontinued. They are 'babyish' and irrelevant; they serve no purpose in adult life.

> I don't think Lessons on the Bible are necessary because when you go to work we forget all about the days when we were at school and had Bible lessons.

> I cannot see the use of having lessons on the Bible. When we start work the boss doesn't want to know what you were in the R.I. test, and it is not a thing that crops up in everyday life.

When we turn to the comments on the method of religious instruction, we find much the same story. A few like it as it is, a few want to get rid of it, and the vast majority would like to see more discussion, more give and take, and a greater relevance to daily life.

We must put into the first group the child who says enigmatically,

> I like being taught thinks.

He is probably one of those who are afraid of the pointlessness and lack of direction of a bad discussion.

> Discussions are interesting, but then they would get boring and there would not be much taught.

It is clear that some of the children have experienced uncontrolled discussions where those who like to air their views, often woolly and ill-founded, do so at the cost of those who would like to be instructed more authoritatively. One supporter of more discussion, indeed, unwittingly reveals that a bad discussion is less valuable than a good lesson in which the teacher makes the whole class co-operate.

> I think discussing the subject is more interesting because if you don't want to join in you don't have to.

Others point out that discussion lessons are always shared enthusiastically by the same group, and some are always silent. Another expressed the view that it is difficult to discuss until you understand more fully and know more of the subject.

A warm welcome for more discussion comes from four fifths of the papers. Some regard it as a change from a monotonous method.

> I would like to have a discussion instead of writing and listening to the teacher all the time.

I would like to see more discussing than just writing on the board and copying it down blindly.

Others are obiously left uncomprehending by their present instruction, and would like to clear things up by talking them over.

I think I would be better if we didn't do so much writing but discussed the bible more often I would more likely be able to understand it better then as I think it is hard to understand.

I think by talking about Religen I clears the douts and forms defanat idears.

I think it is best to discuss thinks in scripture because you understand more.

Some of them chafe against the authoritarianism of overmuch instruction:

I could not agree more with the point of discussing the point and not just be told that so and so was right and he was wrong and you should do this and that. Discussing the point is what I and want and will do.

In one case, this irritation is represented as undermining faith:

It makes me disbelieve in God more when we are taught the same drooy speech every week.

The point is most fairly and frankly put by one of the children who have now, in their last year, begun to hold discussions in class:

Before last year I began to think of R.I. Lessons as uninteresting we were told things out of the Bible and we just had to accept them as true. (It was hard luck if we had our doubts.) But now we've reached our 4th year we can discuss, and I am sure when I say that I am not the only one, who now looks forward to them.

One of the elements in the desire for discussion is entirely admirable: the determination to 'have it out' with the teacher. Mere instruction can miss its mark in two ways: it may be too difficult or it may not ask enough. Some complain of its difficulty: 'the teacher puts too much into our head we arent old enough to understand even if we are 15', and 'I believe that too much of this is being pumped into us ... Let the people think their own ideas up'. Others point to the passivity of the over-instructed class:

Most scripture lessons at the lower end of the school are given by the teacher doing all the work, and the class just sitting back and relaxing.

Both these criticisms would be met by the kind of class described here:

> I like a scripture lesson when you are at ease with the teacher, when you argue and have it out with the teacher about certain points. I like to have debates about unexplainable things to get nearer to the truth.

If we read between the lines that our critics write, remembering their cautionary remarks that discussion can be a waste of time, and that discussion needs preliminary knowledge, but remembering too the weight of opinion against repetitiveness and monotony, we begin to see that they are most of them in all seriousness asking for a class in which the teacher is ready to teach, but to teach what they begin to feel the need of learning; to present the message of the Bible in relation to the issues of the present moment, and then to wait, open and friendly—'at ease'—for the class to 'have it out' and to try to 'get nearer to the truth'. Some just want to talk:

> It is most interesting to voice your opinions in a discussion.

But the desire is overwhelming for something that represents an open situation, in which the teacher does not abdicate either his initiative or his authority, but uses them to discover what is going on in the minds of his class, and then to take them demonstrably, palpably, sensibly, 'nearer to the truth'. What this can mean, we must now begin to consider, but these testimonies are powerful in their injunction that we must make it mean something. Two thirds of our children declare themselves dissatisfied with the religious instruction they now receive.

What can be done to meet them?

Note: The Consistency of the Comments

A somewhat unexpected feature of the children's answers was the degree of personal consistency they revealed. On most of the papers, the first answer set the tone for the rest, distinguishing not only between downright orthodoxy and agnosticism, but between various shades of orthodoxy, and unorthodoxy, and various degrees of critical doubt. It was rare to meet a paper of which one part was in plain conflict with another.

This was not entirely to be foreseen from what is known of adolescents in general. It is customary and necessary to accept from adolescents a measure of inconsistency. They are in process of escaping from the parental pattern of attitude and behaviour, but have not yet had time or seen enough of the world to make their own pattern. This applies, patently enough, to conduct: the immature are capable of callous selfishness and startling generosity within the day. It applies to emotional attitudes, which can range from an unreachable hardness to pulpy sentimentality. And we might expect it to apply, even more, to the shadowy realm of religious speculation and the relatively mature task of forming a coherent philosophy of life.

These youngsters, indeed, may be thought to be in advance of their parents in attaining a consistent point of view. The *Puzzled People* survey discovered that about a quarter of their observed group held beliefs which are rationally incompatible. A quarter of the regular churchgoers denied the divinity of Christ, while a quarter of the agnostics accepted it while denying the existence of God. A sixth of the agnostics accepted the doctrine of the Virgin Birth. Our young people show no sign of such irrational confusion. They are muddled in their thought, unsuccessful in their expression, but they either know where they stand or know that they do not know.

Here, for example, is a pious girl, who reveals that she is a Catholic, and shows in all her comments the kind of accepting, undisturbed faith towards which Catholic instruction is directed. Dealing with 'The Bible's not forced to be true' she is firm—'I disagree'—without being unaware of the difficulty: 'although it has got a point'. She sees that this issue is not to be settled on its own ground alone, but is an element in a whole view of the universe:

> But I think to believe the bible you must have faith in God.

These three marks, assurance, awareness, and the appeal to the roots of faith, reappear:

> I think that Jesus Christ was physically the same as us only unlike us he led a Holy life, and was born of God. When he was twelve he must have been very intelligent for he asked many questions in the temple, and surprised the Scribes and the Doctors.

Her appeal to evidence shows that she is aware of a problem but her own certainly appears in her flat affirmatives: 'he led a Holy life and was born of God'. So with the rest:

I think that God is just and wise. He is good because when we ask for our sins to be forgiven we know they have been.

Yes, I think Christianity is worth dying for . . .

No, I don't think it is boring to be good. I don't think anyone's perfect. I think goodness comes from the heart, and it's much pleasanter to be nice, and when you start work no ones going to employ a person with a bad reputation, and I think you have many more friends if you kind.

She believes in heaven, she accepts suffering as partly the conse-quence of free will, partly a condition of life in which God shares: '

I think God feels the pain as much as we do.

She believes in prayer, and is willing to take no for an answer. And, most significant of all, because here is an issue on which she would not have been instructed, she takes up the same 'accepting' attitude to her scripture lessons:

I think the lessons we have help us to understand more about God. Each time I learn something new and wonderful. I don't think the Bible's ever old because some of the things we read happen in everyday life. I like the Scripture lesson where we sit and listen to the teacher and ask questions on what we don't understand. I wouldn't like it to be like a debate because you usually get one person who doesn't believe in God and who keeps asking the same question, 'Can you prove it?'

The extreme contrast with this is offered by a perfervid ration-alist who will have no truck with anything in the Christian scheme. Two of her ample paragraphs must suffice:

The Bible is a collection of stories and as such they make interesting reading BUT the facts contained therein *CANNOT* possibly be true. The writers of the books in the Bible were so completely taken in by Jesus, who, I admit, was a very clever *MAN (HE HAD NO SUPERHUMAN POWERS WHATSOEVER)* that they literally let their pens and their imaginations run away with them. Even today one reads, usually in the Sunday papers, about the hundreds of weak-willed extremists who are completely taken in by the people who claim that they possess unnatural powers. Such people were the Disciples, Prophets, etc.

And, on the creation:

GOD DID NOT MAKE THE WORLD BECAUSE
a. There is, in my belief, no God.

b. In 1830 Lyell's 'Principles of Geology' and in 1859 Darwin's 'Origin of Species' completely disproved Genesis.

c. Scientists have now established the fact that the Universe began as a small particle of gas matter. From whence that came is not, at this time, known. However, everyday a new fact or an unknown thing is invented or discovered and in time, perhaps millions of years in the future, it will be discovered from where the gas matter came. The story, the fiction story, of God making the world was established due to man's incapability to explain the world's creation. Man likes to think that he knows everything and so he invented this God as a simple solution to it all.

From this stronghold she demolishes every proposition with the same weapons. Jesus was a clever man 'backed by some equally clever friends, his propaganda agents'. The image of God presents no problems because 'there is no God'. Dying for Christianity would be ridiculous:

> The idea of living is to carry on the human cycle, to get married and to have children.

And so with heaven:

> a fictitious wonderland created by some of our more imaginative brethren.

These two statements represent, for fifteen-year-olds, marked consistency; but then, it may be argued, these two points of view are relatively simple to maintain, and may both represent nothing more than an untroubled acceptance of good teaching from a faithful priest or a rationalist father. Consistency at this level is no cause for surprise. What is more remarkable is the maintenance throughout many of the commentaries of a degree of doubt, of a general disposition to take up a particular stand along with an awareness that such a stand has real difficulties, not yet fully met. The little Catholic was aware that other people felt difficulties, but did not feel them herself: most of our children were still battling within their own minds, and the line of battle appears in all sections of their comments. This may be illustrated from two papers that show subtly different degrees of assurance.

The first is marked by an active faith, taking seriously the difficulties in the religious position, but showing a vigorous determination to hold on to it, with a continual appeal to first-hand experience. 'The Bible', it begins, 'is the history of the Jews in the Old Testament. This was written down as intelligently as they were able. The New Testament tells the stories of Christ, who some of the Jews thought was the Messiah'. The tone of this comment is more significant than its content. 'Of course', it seems to be saying, 'yes, of course there may be historical errors in the Bible, distortions of fact, and difficulties of interpretation; but that is no reason for not taking it seriously.' 'And of course', it goes on 'there is mystery in the Biblical account of creation, but then mystery lies behind the scientific account as well.'

> Science has tried to prove that everything evolved from a speck of protoplasm, but who put the protoplasm there? We call him God. The earth was pulled off the sun they say. This I think is true but it is no accident.

And so the argument continues, appreciating the reasonableness of scepticism, but claiming equal reasonableness for the Christian claims:

> Jesus Christ could have been this ('an ordinary man') but he was perfect in his ways and if the best of people try to be good they fail so I think he was God in human form.

A defence of prayer combines real experience with a somewhat unusual explanation:

> Prayer is useful for if in doubt and no one to ask God, he will tell you in maybe a dream. I have found this. After puzzling over a problem one night I went to bed and awoke with the answer.

The writer's experience of what must be an unusually vigorous church enables her to deal decisively with the problem of church-going:

> Nonsense, when I go to church young practically run it, there are about two thirds of the members below the age of 25.

Finally, as we should expect, she favours discussion in class:

> It is more interesting if you can discuss for different opinions are expressed and the matter is sometimes reversed from the teacher's point of view to the pupils.

In the next paper we can see a greater degree of doubt: a sense almost of dismay before such issues as the validity of the Bible or the nature of God, combined with a practical goodwill towards effective Christianity. 'Some of the Bible is true and some is false', because 'it is a record handed down'. The creation story is impossible to accept.

I cannot believe that something that isn't physical can create moun-
tains, seas, animals, etc. . . . You cannot get something out of nothing, and I think there was an earth when God started, if He ever did.
Jesus Christ was an ordinary man, and God is simply incompre-
hensible.

I used to imagine God as something like that but now I am getting
muddled and I dont know what he's like.

But 'it is not boring to be good', nor would it be dull if everybody 'was good and cheerful', for 'the more bad you are the more
trouble you find yourself in'. Unexpectedly, he claims to believe
in heaven and hell, but is not much concerned about them.

I think one life on earth is enough to thank God for and you should
try and be perfect in that life.

Prayer is 'good, because it helps to solve some of your problems'. Church-going can be lively: 'What about the Harvest Festival
or the Christmas Festivals or organised rallies?'; and scripture lessons should be improved with progressive bible-teaching and more
discussion.

Finally, without comment, here is a cry *de profundis:*

The Bible	there is a lot of rubis in it techers abmit ther is so that I do not think that it is true.
Creation	I think that it is a lot of Hill Billi nonsens that is no true.
Jesus Christ	I bont think Jesus heuled eney boby.
God	I carnt amagin anibody in the sky.
Sacrifice	I wood not dye for christianity its just Daft dyeing for Christianity.
Boring to be Good?	Yes and No.
Heaven	How Do I now theres a heaven or you I Dot think there a heaven.
Suffering	('God couldn't care for us') God Daft I think that has one is true.
Prayer	Just a wast of time Prayer.
Church-going	I Dont go to Church Dont like Church.
Scripture lessons	Lessons on the Bible are the same all your life Verey Bul.

Reading these papers, and the hundreds more that are similarly
self-consistent in tone and attitude, presents a strong impression
that these children are thinking for themselves, and beginning to
occupy a view-point of their own. If a child has a clear Christian

outlook on one issue, we may expect him to show it in another; an agnostic is a thorough-going agnostic; and a degree of open-mindedness will reveal itself in all situations; a muddle over one problem will be paralleled by the same sort of muddle over another. Relatively few children merely follow the lead given by the questionnaire, few merely parrot a parent or a teacher.

It is not suggested that the positions at which the children have arrived are intellectually coherent and without self-contradiction. The heresy-hunters will sniff out grave implications in the most orthodox papers; the militant atheist will be vexed by the widespread belief in prayer. But we cannot escape the sense that here we are dealing with people who have begun to accept or reject teaching, to interpret experience and to speculate about the mystery of life from an individual patch of ground where they feel their feet or are conscious that they are unsure. The particles of their thought are beginning to crystallize into structure, their minds are beginning to have a 'view'.

It thus becomes of prime importance that their education should be conducted 'within the view'. What they are asked to look at must be something they are already prepared to see, something within their line of vision, even though it may be further away than they have been accustomed to look. They may be asked to raise their eyes, but we cannot expect them to turn their backs on what they have already seen for themselves. Meaning, even the eternal truth, comes through what has already been found to be true, even when the discovered truth is so small a part of the whole that it is really false.

CHAPTER THREE

THE JUDGEMENT CONSIDERED

WHAT are we to make of all this? How far may we be encouraged by what these children say? What have they learnt, and of what value is it?

Certain encouraging features stand out at once. These fourteen-year-olds are interested in religious issues. When we have made all allowances for the fact that they were told to talk and write, and that children in school usually do what they are told, it is still clear that here they were engaged on a congenial task. Any teacher who has tried to provoke a discussion in English or History will perceive that the discussions 'went' with a genuine life and vigour. Any teacher who has collected up compositions on *Spring* or *Patriotism* or *A Railway Station* will recognize that the comments on our papers come from people who have something to say. Our quotations were the briefest that made their point: the longer ones convey more vividly than these the general readiness to respond.

Furthermore, they have been interested for some time. The questions we posed were, after all, extensive in their range: the existence and nature of God, the divinity of Christ, eternity, sacrifice, ethics, educational method. These are not issues to which we should expect much prior attention from the gang of schoolboys whom we see tumbling off the school bus. Yet the confidence and eagerness with which they attack our questions, the rarity of the confession, 'I have not thought much about this', the air, so frequently noticeable, of 'I have an answer to that one', the frequency of those answers that try to find a reason why other people believe differently ('they like to believe the hard way', 'they want something to lean on', 'invented by the priests . . .')—all this conveys an impression that thought has been going on and minds have been at work.

Inescapable, too, is the note of sincerity. Our little agnostics are wholly delightful in their confident denials, our little Christians very moving in their honest shrinking from the ultimate sacrifice ('I personally would not dye . . .', 'I would go on living because you can still be a Christian inside'). They may be following the line taken in their home, but nevertheless they are demonstrably taking a stand. There is no trace here of the desire to say the correct thing, so familiar to those who read essays by sixth formers.

The freshness and warmth of the children's discussion comes with a certain unexpectedness if we accept the common view that 'R.I.' must be an unpopular subject; but not if we take into account wider studies of adolescence. Fifteen for girls, sixteen for boys, are commonly found to be the peak ages for religious conversions of the 'critical' kind that can be pinned down to a particular event, [1] and those who experience no sudden conversions report the middle teens as a period of decision, either to continue in or reject the framework of belief which they had inherited. An interest in the intellectual problems posed by a religious faith begins to appear at a mental age of twelve; so that highly intelligent children begin to 'doubt' before they are ten, and the less able at thirteen or fourteen. A study of religious conflict between the beliefs of childhood and adult doubt found evidence that this was generally resolved by twenty, after a peak period of struggle at seventeen. Beliefs about particular religious propositions change radically between twelve and eighteen. Most twelve-year-olds believe in hell; most eighteen-year-olds do not. Most twelve-year-olds believe that to be a Christian one must go to church; most eighteen-year-olds believe that churchgoing is not necessary. Most twelve-year-olds believe that every word in the Bible is true; most eighteen-year-olds do not. Groups of students report that most of them underwent a period of rebellion or doubt about their religious upbringing in adolescence, the median age being 15½ for men, 14½ for women.

Not only these specific enquiries into religious interests, but the more general studies of adolescent attitudes would also indicate a readiness to take religion seriously. This is the time for moving

---

[1] Billy Graham's 12,000 converts in 1954 were mostly clustered round the age of fifteen.

from dependence on parents to inter-dependence with one's peers, when home values and peer-group values come into conflict, and father and father's faith or unfaith come under scrutiny. At the same time, the human community into which the adolescent is about to plunge is now seen to be less manageable, less predictable, than it seemed in childhood. The peer-group itself may still offer a certain familiarity, but the working world, the busy strangers who have begun to stand out from the meaningless crowd, are unknown, vaguely threatening factors in a situation with which the youngster is soon to have to deal. Even the peer-group presents its problems, with its pressure towards a conventional conformity in dress and entertainment, values and feelings, sorely vexing to the child who has felt himself to be uniquely valued in the home situation. The adolescent thus develops a sense of unease that we may easily exaggerate but which, if we underestimate it, seals us off from the possibility of understanding or comfort.

At the centre of this lies the unspoken question, 'Am I normal? Am I unique?' In the healthy family, the child is assured of a comfortable answer to both these questions. He is the child who is wanted for his normal childishness and his unique individuality. He fulfils expectation: he is at once the type and the special case. But in the new, horizontal situation of adolescence, he finds his uniqueness a problem: his size, his voice, his lack of skill, his failure to respond to what other apparently more confident youngsters are deeply moved by. And so the unframed question stirs beneath his experiments in conduct, his sudden fanaticisms, his hero-worship and his cynical withdrawals: Who am I? and who are they?

This is at root the religious question: 'What is man that he should be clean?' 'How should man be just with God?' 'What is man that thou art mindful of him?' These are not the academic questions of a scripture lesson: they are the questions that man asks because he is man, and that the young must ask as they become men. And when our children say 'I have often been puzzled by this' they are speaking the truth about their condition.

To this extent, then, the discussions we report reflect a natural healthiness and vigour, a general interest in a matter of importance. When we go beneath this vague responsiveness to the quality and content of the responses made, we find the situation much more difficult to assess. Some features are healthy enough: the presumption that the world ought to be 'fair' and the deep feeling behind the protests against its unfairness; the feeling that the world ought to make sense; the disposition towards prayer; the constructive criticism of scripture teaching. Some may take comfort from the apparently widespread acceptance of orthodox ideas; there is more acceptance here of traditional language and symbolism than we should find in a corresponding adult group. This is confirmed by other studies; but these also confirm that the orthodoxy will not last. Studies of youngsters just before and just after leaving school make plain that the young worker soon gives up the scriptural imagery that a year or so earlier he was content to use. The number of our children who use it is thus of no great significance: they will soon be fewer.

Indeed, when we begin to think of what awaits these youngsters in the next two years, and ask how far their present achievement is likely to wear under the strains of a new life, we may be tempted to judge the picture very dark. Despite their high concern, and the integrity of their point of view, these young people show little sign of a constructive framework of thought and intelligible belief. They have a site, but no house: what is to happen when they leave the shelter of home and school?

For it is no puritan rigorism that adjudges the environment lying in wait for them to be largely hostile to the growth of serious purpose and the flowering of conscience. The inner nature from which high aspiration springs 'is not strong and overpowering and unmistakable, like the instincts of animals. It is weak and delicate and subtle and easily overcome by habit, cultural pressure and wrong attitudes towards it'. [2]

How will this stand up to the pressures from what Richard Hoggart[3] describes as the Candy-floss World, in which 'Everybody's Doing It Now', Sex in Shiny Packets, Scepticism without Tension? The boys will soon be plunged into equality with older men, in a world of bawdy talk, horse-play, gambling, drinking, a narrow world in which life becomes routine—'Work, sleep, work, sleep, with some beanos until you're dead—"one dam' thing after another"—so that the world is "dull rather than naughty".' The philosophy of the young worker is a philosophy of hedonism, of sturdy self-reliance and good-humoured tolerance, and consequently of indifference to any authority without teeth ('If you think it's all right, it's all right; how do they know better than we do?'). There

[2] A. H. Maslow, *Motivation and Personality* (Harper, New York, 1954).
[3] *The Uses of Literacy* (now in Pelican Books).

is equally sturdy self-assertiveness in a competitive situation ('If you don't look after yourself nobody will. You've got to be a bit cheeky to get on'). The girls working for their brief spell in a more protected environment will spend much of their working hours yearning for the easy gaiety of the evening, or retailing its delights next morning.

In all this those who do not go to church—and they will be the vast majority—will have no stimulus to continue the exploration they have so promisingly begun. 'I often wonder about that' will become 'I used to wonder about that, but I don't any more.' The weak and delicate inner nature will be, only too easily, overcome. This does not mean the end of conscience and decency; but it does mean that, to quote Hoggart again, 'the sense of the nearness of personal horizons and of the folly of expecting too much' will make them 'not merely unfanatic but unidealistic.'

It is this threat from the immediate future that makes so urgent a sober judgement on the readiness of our youngsters. 'Unto him that hath shall be given'; but have they achieved enough to give promise of gaining more? Have they even grasped enough to keep, or will even that which they have be taken away?

Before we can answer this question, we must be as clear as we can about what we may expect to achieve by the age of fifteen, with children in a maintained school, that must operate outside the corporate life of the church, in a society whose mind is so open, as Chesterton observed, that it never shuts on anything. There has been little full-dress appraisal of the aims—the realistic, realizable aims—of religious education in the public system of education; [4] and those who seek to fulfil the charge laid on them have had to skirmish in a no-man's land between the full Christian commitment sought by the Church and the vague 'spiritual values'—a kind of tepid course of ethical vitamins—that raise two cheers at educational conferences. Most teachers of 'R.I.' have had at some time or other to withstand the pressure to turn themselves into the guardians of the school's morals ('Why can't you teach 4B not to cheat?'). But this is not their primary business. Religion is first of all about the roots of the spirit: the fruits, though they need attention, come only when the roots have struck into the soil.

But if the Christian is not content to turn religion into ethics, he is, on the other hand, unable to adopt wholesale the educational

---

[4] Though see W. R. Niblett, *Christian Education in a Secular Society* (OUP, 1959).

programme of the church. It is appropriate for a Catholic school to make its children learn a creed they do not fully understand, because later there will be continuing guidance from a priest in its interpretation and relevance to the raw realities of life. It is equally appropriate for a Quaker school to postpone until maturity the discussion of the larger problems of belief, and to rely in the early years on the awakening of a sense of unity with the life of the community. Any denomination can plan its work on the assumption that seeds sown in childhood may ripen to harvest in adult life. Tares and wheat may be left to grow together if one day there is to be a reaping. But any plan for long-term religious education of this kind, demanding the laying of foundations for later building, must include an active promotion of responsible church membership: and this is precisely what the maintained school cannot do without getting embroiled in denominational difficulties. It can of course, enunciate the principle that Christianity is in its very nature corporate; it can make use of local churches for services for leavers, on speech day, at Christmas; but it cannot itself be an organic part of the life of the church.

It therefore becomes necessary to advance a theory of religious education which corresponds to the actual rôle, and not the rôle that Christians might hope it would fill. Christians are free to persuade, to offer their criticism of social and political trends, to press for action and to propagate ideals. But in doing so they must respect the personal integrity of other members of the community: they must make their appeal on open ground accessible to rational examination and confutation. They may convince but they may not subdue. They may challenge response but they may not simply demand allegiance. They may seek to lead, but their leadership must be a showing of the way and not a subjugation of the led.

The problem this creates for religious education is that children can easily be subjugated, but they cannot be expected to see the way, for the very choice of ways is hidden in the future. They can be confirmed in the church membership into which they were born, but they cannot be convinced of a view of life before they know what life is like and before their mind is large enough to grasp the issues involved. They cannot truly respond until they are responsible, free to make a real response. Adolescent conversions represent a genuine desire to respond, but they are emotional rather than intellectual or truly volitional; and though within the continuing Christian community an emotional shift may be acceptable as a preparation for later growth, it cannot be acceptable as an object of education in the maintained school. If Christians were to announce to the nation's parents that they proposed to work the emotions of their charges in the hope that their intellects would later fall into line, they would soon forfeit their opportunity of doing anything at all.

The defence of Christian education must be made to rest on the same open ground as that of all our education: it must seek to perform some task which would be accepted as *healthy*, contributing to wholeness of the personality, and would not be judged by the conscientious agnostic to be limiting or hampering. Education offers an enlargement of personal horizons, in the understanding that there is more to the world than the untutored eye perceives, and in the learning of skills by which men and women respond in greatness. Religious education, too, must be concerned with the enlargement of personal horizons, with what there is to be seen beyond the obvious, and with the power of the seeing eye. Faith, wrote the schoolboy, means believing what you know isn't true. Faith, wrote Dean Inge, is the resolution to stand or fall by the noblest hypothesis. Our religious education must side with the Dean rather than the schoolboy; for none, even in a secular society, will cavil at the presentation of a creative vision.

The 'open' defence of the presentation of the Christian world view is not that it is 'true' (which merely means that Christians say it is true, and is therefore, in an open society, tautological) but that it is 'larger' than any other view. We are all materialists in the sense that the obvious realities seem both obvious and real. But then we are all pre-copernican in the sense that as far as we are concerned the sun goes round the earth. And as the scientist has enlarged our pre-copernican assumptions, so the Christian seeks to enlarge our material assumptions. Merely to ask the question 'Did God create the world?' is to push out horizons, for it raises at once the other question: 'Or did the world just happen?' To ask, 'Is Jesus divine, and does he represent an intention of God for humanity?' is to raise the other question: 'Or may man be just what he pleases?' And to consider the doctrine of the Holy Spirit is to ask: 'In the apparent hopelessness of the human predicament is there really hope or is there really no hope?'

No theory of education can stand which rules out the possibility of these questions being raised; no one can believe that a man is the worse for having faced them; and no one can object to the search for nobility among the grand hypotheses of the human mind. What *can* be objected, by the conscientious agnostic, is that while children are too young to judge, they should not be indoctrinated in such a way as to reduce their powers of judgement in the years to come. But this is no argument against including in the school curriculum the Christian view of man and his meaning. No one can be the worse for having met it: to meet it squarely is an exercise in freedom. Even on the narrowest libertarian grounds, a man is free to choose only if he knows what he chooses between.

This argument does not constitute an attempt to find a highest common factor among all shades of opinion in the community, by way of producing a harmless, universal syllabus of religious instruction that no one can object to. It is an attempt to clear the grounds on which a Christian must stand if he is to be honest in his acceptance of the charge laid upon him. This he must do, not merely because he lives in an open society, with no more authority than that society confers upon him, but because his duty as a teacher is first to the children under his care. These children are soon to be men and women, out in the open society; and if when they arrive there, they find themselves on totally different ground from where they stood in school, they will abandon everything they stood by.

The common ground between the two worlds, of school and life, is to be found in the continuing growth of the child's personality. In the adult world it is a man's business to be a person; in school it is the child's business to mature. The secondary school child is well aware of this, and seizes eagerly on any opportunities of acquiring such knowledge and skill as demonstrably add to his personal stature and give promise of adult effectiveness. Vocational interest runs high because the boy sees himself as a worker instead of a dependant, or the girl sees herself in her home. Problems of etiquette and personal relations assume importance because the youngster is about to be responsible for his own effectiveness. And as any sixth form teacher knows, there is an interest ready to be awakened in the ideas of adult life, often appearing as a snobbish interest in the U and non-U of the intellectual world, but yet to be recognized as important, a uniform to be worn even if not yet a true garment of the soul.

What the adolescent is asking is to be brought up against the kind of thought that will help him to maturity, to know the kind of question that men ask, to practise thinking as men think, and to gain the insight into his own condition and the human condition at large, that a man must have if he is to stand without fear. It is this that lies beneath the desire of our commentators for a more 'adultish' treatment of religion and their satisfaction when they get it. 'We don't always learn about the Bible, but other things which grown-ups discuss.' They are right to want it, and it is the school's business to provide it.

But this particular commentator was wrong in implying that the Bible is not a 'thing which grown-ups discuss'. The case for scripture teaching rests on the fact that the Bible treats of the great themes that truly mature adults must discuss. There are three fields of thought and experience which a mature person must enter with his eyes open, which as a child he could afford to ignore. He must understand something of the nature of other human beings, their needs and dreams, so that he can act responsibly towards them, and win response from them to himself; he must understand something of his own nature, because he can no longer leave the control of it to others; and he must find some sort of meaning in the chaos of experience, for he can no longer live at second hand with the selection of experience provided by his parents and teachers. In other terms, the mature person must deal for himself with problems of human relationships and ideals, problems of personal responsibility, and problems of meaning.

This is substantially the picture that emerges from G. W. Allport's study of personality[5] in which he describes three 'marks of maturity'. 'First,' he says, 'a variety of interests which concern themselves with ideals, object and values ... Second, the ability to objectify oneself, to be effective and insightful about one's own life ... Finally, some unifying philosophy of life, not necessarily religious in type, nor articulated in words, nor entirely complete. But without the direction and coherence supplied by some dominant integrative pattern any life seems fragmented and aimless.'

If we accept these 'marks of maturity' as broadly valid, they enable us to see more clearly the significance of religious education, which becomes a means of promoting a mature religion. In so far as the Bible and the witness of the Church are concerned with the human condition, in its loneliness and its community, and are presented in such a way as to contribute to maturity, they can be defended with confidence as a direct meeting of the needs of adolescence.

[5] *The Individual and His Religion* (Constable, 1951), p. 59.

The special task of the secondary school may be defined as an examination of religious concepts, directed towards the shedding of infantile forms and the acceptance of adult ones. This would at once cut through most of the difficulties aired by our young critics, as it does the more searching objections of older critics. For as Allport later observes, 'Most of the criticism of religion is directed to its immature forms.'[6] This is certainly true of Freud's attack upon it. Religion, he argues, is an infantile fixation. It is a means whereby men and women dream out their unfulfilled desires, escape from their own conflicts, and shirk the realities of the world. It is true that the immature will use their religion in this way, as they will use anything else, from film stars to sex; but this does not mean that religion is itself an illusion, any more than film-stars or sex are illusions. The business of the school is to encourage growing-up, in religion as in everything else: to face in a mature manner the ultimate issues of an adult life.

At this point some teachers may call to mind the classes they teach, skylarking happily before the lesson begins, and thereafter bored and listless, or giggling and inattentive, unpredictable in their spelling, shallow in their judgements, and unresponsive to difficult or unfamiliar ideas; and may wonder if this talk of maturity is relevant. Is fourteen the beginning of maturity? Or is it merely the low tide of childhood, 'standing water, between boy and man'? On this view, religious education could be no more than a *preparatio evangelica*. The task of the school would be the passing on of a body of religious knowledge, along the lines of the Agreed Syllabuses, in the hope that when maturity is reached it would be available as a built-in frame of reference for the understanding of the human condition.

The practical difficulty in this view is that children forget most of what they learn at school unless it is used soon after it is learnt. Even a skill, such as literacy, is lost if it is not practised; and knowledge disappears more rapidly and more inevitably. This is peculiarly true of knowledge that was unusable when it was acquired. The research that has gone into the forgetting of nonsense syllables has its lessons for the scripture teacher: if his work does not 'make sense' it will soon be forgotten.

The problem may thus be restated. Instead of asking if our children are mature, we may ask: 'Can religion "make sense" at the age of fourteen?' And to this question, our commentaries seem

6   *Op. cit.*, p. 60.

to provide an encouraging answer. The majority of these children are demonstrably busy 'making sense' of religious propositions. They may come to different 'senses', and their effort is woefully ill-informed; but their eager search for a way out of a problem is a mark of the maturing mind.

The work of Piaget, which may well be the most fruitful line of study for the education of personality, shows how children move from one attitude of unquestioning acceptance of the rules of the game, whether marbles or morals, into an autonomous period when the rules may be changed to suit changed conditions. The child who moves satisfactorily into the autonomous phase, however, sees that the rules have a 'point'. In the case of marbles, this change may take place at the age of seven; and when once the shift has occurred it is soon demonstrated in more serious and complex matters.

By fourteen, then, we may expect children—even less able children—to be capable of this 'autonomy' in religious ideas. They are ready to take hold of them in their own way, provided that they see their point. The problem then is not 'Are they ready for an adult presentation of religion?' but 'Has an adult religion any point for a fourteen-year-old? Is his experience the kind of experience on which religious ideas throw light? Is there any connexion between the condition of the adolescent and the condition of man as seen in the Bible?'

To answer this question we first proceeded empirically by asking some teachers to tell us what problems in their own condition their children were most concerned about. What are the things that seem most to arouse them in discussion? In what direction does a red herring in class most frequently turn? We were given the following answers.

They are worried about relations with parents and, to a lesser extent, with teachers. How far ought they to do what they are told, to conform to what often seem unnecessary restrictions, to 'be good'? Or must they, in the words of our commentaries, 'be cheeky in order to get on'? Any parent, indeed any adult who remembers his adolescence, will recognize that this is a genuine area of trouble, sometimes painful, sometimes merely irritating or calling for wariness, but always present as school life draws to an end. The shift from dependence on parents to the complex relation with other adults and the peer-group must always present its difficulties. It is not a simple move from one dependence to another: it is the end of dependence and the beginning of an uncertain mixture of dependence, independence and interdependence. We cannot desire it to be made easy, for it is the situation in which a nursling achieves his weaning and cuts his teeth. Furthermore, it is a problem that remains in adult life. We do not settle, once for all, the problem of authority. The adult carries with him for life his moral inheritance from his parents, and must needs use it in interpreting the impact of employers and work-mates, wife and husband, and even the imperative authority of his helpless infant. In facing this claim of other authorities upon his will, the adolescent is thus performing more than a passing task of his development: he is engaging in a complex struggle that will remain with him when he is a grandfather.

The second field of anxiety lies within the area of the peer-group, where problems arise in three forms: snobbery, friendship and sex. By snobbery, adolescents mean the indifference and repulses they meet from those of their age-group who close up against their advances. Membership of the current set is a highly prized possession: membership of *some* set is a desperate need. Yet the sociometrists tell us that a tenth of the average school class are isolates, and thirty percent are either isolates or 'fringers', people whom nobody wants as friends, and whose nervous, and consequently clumsy attempts to attach themselves to the crowd will probably be rebuffed.

A single close friendship will mitigate this general social ineffectiveness, but the break-up of a friendship may rob popularity of its savour. Into the making and losing of friends goes a strong current of adolescent feeling, and the irrational, ill-founded quarrels, the pathetic little revenges, the awkward bids for attention, the deep sulkiness, are expressions of passions that the victim is totally unable to control. Boys, trained to hide their feelings, show less than the girls, but it is likely that they feel as much.

When all this is complicated by sex, as it now is in any class of fourteen-year-olds, the emotional situation is bewildering in the extreme. The young adolescent is nowadays probably better informed than he used to be about the physical facts; but for the emotional onslaught of advertising, entertainment and the gutter press he is totally unprepared. Our culture speaks of sex with two voices: one, out of the past, repeating its chill formulas in favour of chastity, the other, eager and contemporary, sowing by word and song and picture the seeds of desire. At the same time adults have chosen to relinquish their right of supervision, and leave their adolescents to find their own way in a country where there are now two sets of maps. The problem is not a simple conflict between desire and self-control: it is a radical uncertainty about how to demonstrate one's personal adequacy. The sex rôle is the most deeply personal rôle we ever have to fill, searching out our image of ourselves at its most physical and its most spiritual at the same time. 'I wish I had a lovely skin,' write the girls to their teen-age journals, 'please can you help me?' 'How can we tell,' ask the boys in their youth clubs, 'when a girl wants us to stop?' 'How can we keep our boy friends,' ask the girls, 'if we don't let them mess about?' [7]

The problems we have considered so far are all aspects of the same conflict over personal relationships, of finding in action a way of making the new bonds of affection and understanding that must now replace the simple bonds of dependence that will no longer serve. Less immediate and less agonizing, but still disturbing and taken seriously, are the problems of personal responsibility that wait in the immediate future: work, money and the use of leisure. By the last year of the secondary modern school, the worker's cares are beginning to look real. For the healthy youngster they are attractive and appealing, but are not without uncertainty and the need for guidance. School leavers are curious about their future situation, eager to reach it, and eager to hear about it. It is probably rare for them to doubt their adequacy here, but they know that they do not know, and are ready, not merely for facts, but for discussion of the personal and moral issues raised by a job in which they will be responsible to others, the control of what seems to them a considerable amount of money, and the use of leisure time that they think they will now be able to call their own.

Within the area of personal responsibility must lie the problem of prayer, with which our young people are so much concerned. They are most of them still praying, in a childish way and with a childish frame of reference. The apparent conflict between prayer and natural law is beginning to press on them, and they are ready to attend to the question 'Does prayer work? and if so, in what way?' If it does, then it becomes a duty. If it is merely a mechanism of self-assurance, then it will soon be abandoned.

7   See J. Hemming, *Problems of Adolescent Girls* (Heinemann, 1960) and
    G. W. Jordan and E. M. Fisher, *Self-Portrait of Youth* (Heinemann, 1955).

cribed as problems
ny do the innocent,
f everything? Here
rowding in on the
: their new reading
stice and fair-play.
em that life needs
piquant and pleas-
well ordered and
that perhaps the

ase about life that
truction should be
solve his personal
his mathematics to
field of interest:

the significance of school studies, the value of different subjects,
the problem of boredom; and behind them the undefined problems
of knowledge and belief, the meaning of proof, the nature and
purpose of God.

We have thus arrived at this list of topics of interest to pupils
of fourteen.

Problems of personal relations:

1 Authority
2 Friendship
3 Sex and marriage
4 Snobbery

Problems of personal responsibility:

5 Money
6 Work
7 Leisure
8 Prayer

Problems of meaning:

9   Suffering
10 Death
11 Learning.

It is a list arrived at by what R. S. Peters calls the analysis of teachers' hunches. [8] Before we make use of it we must ask if it can be validated by more scientific means. The current studies of adolescence make use of categories of 'developmental tasks' which the adolescent most perform in the process of maturing. Havighurst draws up a list of ten, here rearranged in order to bring out the broad correspondence with our list.

Personal relations:

1 Achieving emotional independence of parents and other adults
2 Achieving new relationships with age-mates
3 Achieving a masculine or feminine social rôle
4 Preparing for marriage and family life
5 Desiring and achieving socially responsible behaviour

Personal responsibility:

6 Achieving assurance of economic independence
7 Selecting and preparing for an occupation
8 Accepting one's physique and using the body effectively

Problems of meaning:

9 Developing intellectual skills and concepts necessary for civic competence
10 Acquiring a set of values and an ethical system as a guide to behaviour

Dr Cole's list contains seven:

Emancipation from home control
General social maturity
Interest in the other sex
General emotional maturity
Selection of an occupation
Appropriate uses of leisure
Philosophy of life.

R. G. Kuhlen speaks more broadly of four areas of adjustment: sex-social adjustment and adjustments consequent on attaining

8 See R. S. Peters, *Authority, Responsibility and Education* (Allen and Unwin, 1959). See also R. T. Havighurst and T. Taba, *Adolescent Character and Personality* (Wiley, New York, 1949); L. Cole, *Psychology of Adolescence* (Allen and Unwin, 1948); R. G. Kuhlen, *The Psychology of Adolescent Development* (Harper, New York, 1952).

freedom from parents; vocational adjustment; and ideological adjustment.

No two workers have arrived at exactly the same list, but the general lines they all follow are sufficiently similar to each other and to ours to justify the use of this set of problems in considering the approach to our classes.

Christianity, if it is to be relevant to the life of the teenager, must be seen to bear on these problems, not in a spirit of negation or repression, but in illumination of their meaning and hope of their solution.

CHAPTER FOUR

THE TEACHER'S TASK: A PROBLEM APPROACH

LET us now turn to the practical implications of these reflections. The position we have reached is that we have seen reason to accept the widespread demand for a new approach to religious instruction in the final stages of school life, a decisive and manifest shift of viewpoint, from 'childish' to 'adultish'; and this we take to mean abandoning the familiar 'Bible stories' in favour of a consideration of 'things grown-ups talk about', with the limitation imposed by the fact that some adult themes are too difficult, or too dull, for adolescent discussion. We have in consequence set out ten themes, adult in significance but of peculiar interest to the adolescent, which do not cover all the problems of the human condition, but which are central to the adolescent experience of it. These themes, it is suggested, provide the starting points of religious discourse, grist to the mill of the spirit. The object would be to set out from these themes and to tread out a path from realities to Reality, to show how the immediate problems of living raise, if they are pressed back to their fundamentals, the problem of life.

What is needed is to establish a method that proceeds from the analysis of situations by general principles—what might be described as a Christian technique of problem-solving. Let us try to illustrate this technique by an examination of the first of our themes: the problem of authority.

I · Raising the Problem of Authority

Where a teacher is in good rapport with his class, he will be able to raise some aspect of the conflict with authority that the children are ready to discuss. Does it matter what time you get in at night? Do parents exercise control over where you go in your leisure time? or over what you wear? Do they demand help with the housework? Or a problem may have arisen in school: the difficulties of prefects in dealing with their non-prefect contemporaries, or a new school rule not fully understood. Less direct approaches might make use of a recent case in the newspapers, involving juveniles; a play on television; a film, or a short story read aloud.

Alternatively a situation may be created, and either read in story form or presented dramatically, in a short scene, which may be written and rehearsed, or acted out impromptu from a few hints. 'Marlene and Betty are shop assistants behind the counter early on Thursday morning, busy discussing their plans for the evening off. Marlene is angry because she has been ordered to be home by ten o'clock, since on the previous Thursday she was rather late, and "didn't she 'alf 'ave a row with the old man". Betty is sympathetic, and complains of her mother's fussiness over her activities when she is out: Who does she go with? Are they nice? What do they do?—"As if I couldn't look after myself!". After some discussion a customer interrupts with, "Well, I've heard all *your* troubles. Now listen to mine please. I want a . . ." Marlene is saucy, and the customer stalks out, threatening to write to the manager.'

2 · *Analysing the Problem*

There are two levels of obligation here: obligation at work and obligation at home. These girls and their parents are both 'right' in the sense that the girls need freedom and privacy to sort out their own lives, to exercise their own judgement, and to bear the consequence of their own mistakes, while parents have a duty to be anxious, and to limit freedom that may contain unwarrantable risk. The first step is thus to demonstrate the conflicting points of view, with the object of letting both sides be fully appreciated. Marlene had upset her father by forgetting his situation while she enjoyed her own ('I knew I was all right, didn't I?'); and her father's anger arose because he did not understand her situation. When children dramatize this sort of situation for themselves, and play it out, it is customary for the one who acts the parent-rôle to be surprised herself at what she sees from inside it. 'I never realized they must feel like that about it.'

Then we turn to an analysis of the exact obligations raised here. Coming in 'late' implies some sort of agreement about a reasonable time. How was this agreement arrived at? Would it be imposed by parents? And if so, imposed in full knowledge of what Marlene wanted to do, with a reason given for imposing it? Or was it merely laid down as the 'right' time? Had Marlene really accepted this time, or merely concealed her own intention of ignoring it? In thus discussing a dramatic situation, the children will draw on their own experience of what probably happened; and there should emerge in the discussion the necessity, in any social situation, of an open agreement about obligation, and what it means to both sides.

Then, what of the decision that tonight Marlene must be in by ten? Here is a command laid down clearly: must it be obeyed? This calls for an examination of right and responsibility. A parent has the final responsibility for the well-being of a child at home, and responsibility implies the right to lay down conditions. A child has the 'right' to grow, but this implies freedom over a wide range only when it is exercised responsibly. There is thus a situation in which responsibility is being gradually transferred from parent to child. But is this transfer ever complete? Are we ever really free? This brings in the other level of obligation, to an employer, revealed in the way Marlene and Betty talked so busily that they neglected their customers. Again they were thoughtless of another human being; but they were here also breaking an open obligation which they had accepted when they took the job. So the acceptance of adult status thus involves, at some points, a decrease in freedom, a more nearly absolute obligation.

Is even obedience to an employer an *absolute* obligation? What of an order to cheat a customer or to falsify an account? This raises the problem of conscience viewed as responsibility to more than the immediate persons in a situation. But what is this 'more'? 'Right' and 'wrong' are sometimes easy to distinguish (the girls in the shop, 'wrongly' annoying the customer) but sometimes difficult (settling the 'right' times of coming in at night).

3 · *The Christian Interpretation*

Here the Christian turns to the nature of his belief in God. The *final* authority behind all others is the authority of God. This is an authority 'in the nature of things'. Scientific law is the most obvious example: if you jump off a cliff you will fall to the bottom. Moral law, though less certain, is sometimes equally obvious: if you deliberately try to anger someone, you will make him angry, and this sure consequence has moral implications. We go 'wrong' from ignorance of these laws or from an unwillingness to obey what we know: the laws of hygiene are not yet fully understood, but are often not obeyed even when they are well known. But the Christian believes that notwithstanding our ignorance, these laws are 'there', in the mind of God.

The task of living is thus to find them out. What laws are most important to us? What matters most? The question 'Which is the great commandment?' is just this; and its two-fold answer, the love of God and the love of our neighbour, lights up the situation we have been examining.

Loving God. The idea of God as Father is arrived at by analogy, to express man's discovery about God and the reality of life in terms of what he knows. Examine an ideal family, the best that can be thought: a father who wishes only the happiness and well-being of his wife and children; a mother who loves him and them utterly and unselfishly; and children who have a great deal to learn but feel safe with these loving parents and want to please them. Conflict situations in this family would be certain to be resolved in the end, for every member would set himself to learn the purposes of the others. Such a family does not exist, because parents, though generally wishing well for their children, have limits on their knowledge and patience. But this is the analogy for our understanding of the human situation, and if human beings were to love the Father, in complete whole-person love, they would know that in conflicts of 'rights' there could be found something recognizable as 'right'. They would often disagree on what the 'right' is; but merely to be seeking it changes the situation. Marlene and Betty and their parents were all a little afraid, either for their own rights or their children's safety; but a whole-hearted love makes us unafraid.

Loving your Neighbour. Here again, the analogy of the ideal family gives us insight. In such a family, brothers and sisters would know that they all 'matter' to their parents, and would wish to settle conflicts for each other's benefit as well as their own. They would *wish* to: that is the key to the situation. And so in our normal human relations: if we love God, we wish to behave like a brother to other people. This is not a matter of 'liking' every-body equally, which would be merely absence of taste; but of wishing another's well-being as much as we wish our own. That is what love means to the Christian.

We thus approach all situations in the belief that love is built into them as the supreme obligation; and thus accept the authority of love, the authority of God who is love, in whatever we do.

Here we can turn to biblical situations in which this absoluteness may be seen: the Ten Commandments, an attempt to work out some guiding rules for the expression of love; Amos and Hosea discriminating between religious forms and the demands of conscience; Daniel; Jesus, in the wilderness, in Gethsemane, on the Cross; the teaching of Jesus in the Sermon on the Mount, leading to the concept of the Kingdom of God.

4 · *Application*

Finally, we must examine some larger human situations (industrial conflict, war, refugees, minorities, the colour problem) which may be topical at the time, to show the need for a true understanding of both 'sides', a resolve to find the 'right' between them, and the necessity for an ultimate obedience. The family analogy still holds, and throws light on the situation: a minority must accept some limitations on its 'rights', even while it must demonstrate its rights as part of the total right. And the care for one another implicit in the family is the same care, or concern for another's rights, that reduces tension and makes clear the way to the discovery of 'right'.

It is not expected that this discussion will leave all problems solved. This is implicit in the Christian doctrine that the commandment of love supersedes obedience to rules. Rules may fail in a concrete situation, love illuminates the situation and enables one to tackle it. But such a discussion ought to provide an exercise of conscience and create an awareness of the nature of obligation. Mathematics, after all, is a way of tackling problems, not a ready-made solution: and religious insight is a readiness to see the problem whole, not a set of answers provided by somebody else.

5 · *Teacher and Class*

This discussion of authority has been conducted to illustrate the four clear stages through which all discussions will need to pass. 'Raising the problem' is an attempt to make clear that the incidental difficulties of life are really part of a more general difficulty, and one that can be thought about. The chaotic muddles of conflict with authority are, for most adolescents, merely meaningless irritations, not to be thought about so much as to be felt about and escaped from. And so with all their difficulties, of relations with friends, sex relations, work, money, and the rest, it is a great step forward to discover that these vexations or bewilderments are situations from which one can stand back and secure a temporary point of detachment, can categorize them as aspects of a larger problem to which other human beings have been exposed.

The second stage, the analysis of the problem, involves the discovery of the general in the particular, and the clarification of the difficulty raised by the very generality of it. ('Suppose *everybody always* disobeyed authority just when they felt like it? And suppose *everybody always* obeyed authority however immoral the command?') Problems are not solved by this clarification, but they are restated, removed from the overwhelming private and set in the more manageable public sphere.

The third, the introduction of Christian teaching, presents a new point of view, from which we can glimpse even the general human condition from outside, *sub specie aeternitatis, sub specie crucis.* Here is a decisive restatement of the problem, again not 'solving' it, but setting it in a new light in which a totally different approach can be made.

The last stage offers a return to the concrete, in the wider sphere of human relations, in which it may be seen that the Christian restatement is not merely a matter of private experience, but offers a judgement of group relations in society at large.

Set out in this condensed language, the whole scheme sounds impossibly abstract for a class in a modern school; but there is nothing here that is not already achieved in schools where this method is followed. The range of remarks made here in the first stage could be covered in any class in either discussion or written paragraphs with a minimum of preparation. It is then open to the teacher to raise the key question of stage two: 'Suppose everybody always . . .?' and to guide the discussion along these general lines. The third stage represents familiar teaching material, with no unusual demand except, perhaps, a greater readiness to listen to argument about it than teachers would expect if they were teaching trigonometry. And the final stage demands no more than a readiness to take contemporary and topical material into class.

The unusual and most demanding element in all this is not, indeed, a matter of content, but a new departure in method. The crucial methodological difference between adult and school education lies in the place occupied by discussion. In school it is at best peripheral; with adults it is central. While adults gather quantities of facts and ideas from instruction—lectures, books, broadcast talks, journals—they take hold of the essentials in some sort of exchange, the layman raising his personal difficulty, the two experts bringing their different fields of knowledge together, or the solitary reader working out the private dialogue with which we assimilate new ideas into our own frame of reference. Adult thought is best stimulated and pushed out to the frontiers in open argument, where an idea is bandied about, expressed, re-expressed, from a variety of points of view, and with a variety of emphasis; when more 'abstract' minds are brought into encounter with more 'concrete' ones, and are made to translate their abstractions into realities, or are challenged by the awkward special case; when the relatively unthinking person follows the argument in silence until something clicks into focus, he stumbles on the 'Aha' experience, and, still perhaps stumbling, says what he has seen.

The outcomes of good discussion are various. A fact or an idea is grasped more clearly because it has been viewed from many angles: it stands out solid instead of flat. A mind has been enlarged because it has taken something in, something usable and relevant. A new dimension has been opened up by the discovery that an idea can carry different meanings to different people, and by the insight into the 'otherness' of other people that this brings with it. And a new depth is added to human intercourse, to the slender lines of communication between one human being and another. At its best discussion represents the adventure of the spirit: there is a sense of expectancy, a feeling that anything might happen.

The normal classroom situation is very different. However 'progressive' and project-minded the teacher, he remains the centre of the scene. His object is to help his children to grasp the fact or idea; but this is to be done by simplifying it, by presenting it from one angle, and that the teacher's. He must protect his class from overmuch pressure from 'otherness', and he will rely but little on the ability of children to teach each other—anyone who has set his pupils to correct each other's spelling exercise will know that chaos results. And though good teachers will strive to raise a sense of expectancy, they will wish to keep the adventure under their own control. 'Anything might happen' are joyous words for a child, but for a teacher they are loaded with anxiety.

Now when our commentators speak out so roundly in favour of discussion, they are asking to be allowed to move into this unpredictable, adult situation. They want to come to grips with religious problems in their own way, convinced that they have points to make that must be met; interested in the point of view of their contemporaries; anxious to open up communication with those who are feeling as they are, who have not yet tied everything up.

But before we glibly agree to their demand, we must bear in mind certain conditions of effective adult discussion, and make sure that we can adapt them to the peculiarities of the classroom situation. For any discussion to be profitable the members must be reasonably well-informed, and be faced by specific material to be examined. There must be a subject, and there must be a general competence to deal with it. In personal terms, there must be a leader who knows the subject and can expound it; and members with a sufficiency of understanding to contribute. Progress then demands that the discussion shall be relevant and pointed; widely shared; and in the end, even if not always in the middle, clear as to what it has all been about. Again in personal terms, the leader must guide the discussion to specific points; the members must all contribute, even if no more than simple agreements and disagreements; and the leader may have to recapitulate the main ground that has been covered.

Some parts of this process come more easily to a teacher than others. He is accustomed to expounding a body of knowledge; and it will call for breaking the habits of a life time to hold his knowledge back until it is needed, instead of beginning with it. Nevertheless, the teacher must be ready to teach when the moment comes, and ensure that discussion is not ruined by discursiveness. The child who warned us that 'discussions are interesting but then they would be boring and there would not be much taught' had suffered from uncontrolled debate. To this end, the teacher needs to be more fully and widely prepared than is necessary for a straight lesson. He cannot be content with a set piece—a chapter of the Bible, a journey of St Paul, or the life of a saint, to be 'done' between one bell and the next. He needs to be ready to shift his ground, to twist and turn with the 'rascally fox of an argument' and to know at least the contours of any country in which he may find himself at the end of a gallop. To this question, of the teacher's preparation, we shall have to return.

At the same time, the use of discussion presupposes a class sufficiently well-informed to have something to put into it. Our tape-recordings and commentaries show several favourable signs. These children are interested and ready to talk. They are honest and candid. They represent various points of view, so that almost any issue will divide them, and provoke a lively argument. But they are woefully ignorant of the case they attack and the case they defend. The scientific apologists are so woolly that one wonders what goes on in their science lessons, and their 'world view' seems to comprise little more than a comforting feeling that 'they' have tied everything up and 'we' need do no more about it. The Christian apologists are better informed about their groundwork, but have little idea of the way in which a Christian really sustains his faith. If discussion is to be educative, it is clear that the members of the class will need a new kind of preparation to make use of it.

The progress of the discussion then depends, as we have seen, on being well directed, widely shared, and clearly summarized. The first and last of these offer little problem to an experienced teacher. Experience in questioning yields also skill in the direction of children's questioning; and summing up what has been learnt yields skill in summing up what has been discussed. But it is not easy to outwit the child who likes discussion 'because if you don't want to join in you don't have to'. Expertise in normal teaching techniques becomes almost an obstacle here. A quick question on a matter of fact wakes up the sleeper; but to demand a contribution of opinion from him is to provoke surliness from him and giggling from the rest. Even simple arithmetic is against us here—forty children in a class, forty minutes in a lesson. It cannot be done.

The only satisfactory solution to this problem is to cut the class in two. A group of 15 to 20 is ideal for discussion: small enough to encourage participation, large enough to permit variety of points of view. And if we believe that religious instruction is at least as important as science or cookery, we should be ready to divide our classes as we do in the laboratory or the domestic science room. The laboratory of ideas is at least as demanding as the laboratory of things.

Where this cannot be done, it must be accepted as an inevitable limitation on what can be achieved. Some devices will alleviate the loss, but loss there must be. The large class, as teachers have tirelessly maintained, is the greatest obstacle to true education inherited from the days of cheap education.

The problem of participation itself presupposes the solution of a prior problem: the maintenance of order. As we think of our little blackboard jungles, in which outbursts of primitive behaviour are kept in check only by a continuous exercise of vigilance and will, we may feel that the demand for more 'adultish' treatment carries undertones of irony. It would be foolish to ignore the very real force of this objection. Teachers vary in the sheer power of their personality, as inevitably as they vary in weight. A few, the 'naturals', have simply to enter the classroom to create an atmosphere of concentration and purpose, but most of us, even when accounted 'good disciplinarians', need to develop a strategy of control. And for these it is a bold step to adopt a method whereby some of the initiative passes to the class, and removes the teacher a few vital inches from the emotional centre of the situation.

Here again certain protective techniques may be devised, but when we have made all our plans it must be admitted that success depends on something deeper than plans. It depends on the measure of our resolution 'to stand or fall by the noblest hypothesis'. Within a year these children are to be exposed to risk; and if the school is to give them strength that will last into the new situation, it must be ready to admit the risk to the classroom. It is generally true that the adolescent, half child, half adult, will respond with the half that is appealed to. Treat him as a child and he slips back a few years; treat him as older than he is, and he takes on little extra maturity. The risk is real, but it is a risk worth taking. Furthermore, interesting subject-matter normally reduces the problems of discipline. Novelty heightens attention. Respect evokes respect. And when success comes, it offers the teacher a prospect of an entry into the human situation of the adolescent, where alone the issues of life can be handled with naked hands.

CHAPTER FIVE

THE TEACHER'S TASK: A PROBLEM SYLLABUS

In the last chapter we considered how the problem of authority might be approached from the actual experience of the adolescent. There follow here outlines of possible approaches to the other topics in which the fourteen-year-old is already interested, or can be persuaded to take an interest.

I · *Friendship*

Raising the Problem. The difficulty here is that friendship is at once too intimate and too commonplace to talk about. Many of the pupils will have their 'best friend' with them in class; some may have just quarrelled. The approach needs to be indirect, anaesthetized, either impersonal and generalized or through persons outside the classroom situation.

A general approach might try to get a definition of the word *friend* or *friendship*: 'If you were writing a dictionary, how would you define *friend*?'. Bring out various strands of meaning: liking and loving—*friend* and *free* both come from a word meaning love; shared activities; understanding and open-heartedness; wishing well to the other; being on the same side.

A less abstract approach may be made via rôle-play, three or four pupils acting out an episode in which a young worker stands by a friend who has been caught in an offence, while not himself approving of it, or one in which Suzanne, who likes the theatre, has a chance of seeing a play on an evening that she normally spends with Carole: she breaks the news to Carole and an argument develops. Such situations lend themselves to a letter from one friend to the other, and the class might all try their hands at the letters, a selection of them being read and discussed in the next lesson.

Analysis. The analysis will depend on the way in which the problem has been raised, but the ground to be covered is obvious enough: what we expect of a friend, loyalty and the tension on it when something has gone wrong, we or they have offended, when other people gossip about us; the kind of activity in which friendship grows and is particularly needed; quarrelling and making up; loneliness; numbers of friends, close and less close; the gift of making friends easily and the shyness that prevents it; adult friendships, interrupted by marriage and work. Do we really *make* friends or are they just 'made'? It is often said that a man is known by the company he keeps. This is not always true, and if it were taken too seriously it would be a justification for snobbery; but it contains the element of truth that we are all influenced by and tend to accept the standards of those with whom we spend our time. In what sort of ways do friends influence each other?—the gang, the choice of leisure activities and their influence on character, opinion-forming, values. And so back to 'making friends'. How can we exercise choice without being unfriendly?

The Christian Judgement. Jesus had a group of special friends —the disciples, and among them a few intimates, and Mary and Martha; and he frequently withdrew from the crowd to be with them, or alone in prayer and meditation. But he showed an unfailing friendliness to all he met: the thief on the cross, the prayer for his murderers, the woman taken in adultery, the centurion. Those whose hearts were not large enough to understand his universal friendliness misjudged him here, and accused him of being a friend of publicans, mercenary traitors, and sinners. What they saw as shameful the Christian sees as an ideal, beyond his power to realize, but towards which he is turned as he is filled by the spirit of Christ. For this quality, Christians use the word love, by which they mean, not feeling or sentiment, but the resolve to take another person seriously, to understand his feelings and desires and needs and to respond to them, to meet him and to share his life: an unshakable acceptance of responsibility for another person. This is not natural or easy for us beyond the small circle of our familiar friends, but we learn it as we become aware of the 'friend-ship of Jesus' and discover in his awareness of the Fatherhood of God a sense of the brotherhood of all men. The Cross in an asser-tion that the evil in man's nature, working against friendship, does not break this fact of human interdependence and dependence on God. [1]

Application.   It should be possible to find a conflict in the news at the time, between union and employer, or between two countries or hostile parties, or between black and white. These are rarely open to a simple solution by the injection of mere friendliness, but they may usually be traced to their roots in an absence of the 'other-willing' that the Christian claims is a law of life. The Chris-tian judgement on an industrial or political conflict is most instruc-tive on how it came about. On how the conflict is to be resolved, it is often obscured by economic or procedural technicalities. But even here, the situation would be radically changed if the dis-putants could stand back from the argument and ask: 'What are the *rights* of this situation? What, in particular, are the rights of the other side, which we may be neglecting?' If, instead of sharpening up their own arguments, each side laid themselves open to the arguments of the other side, the conflict would appear utterly different.

When this general ground has been covered, it may be possible to return to the personal situation in which our pupils are involved, and to let them lead the discussion into their own problems. The most intimate friendship is enriched, the most painful quarrel is mitigated, by a new entry of the imagination and the will from the other person's side. And when this happens, we recognize the Spirit of God.

2 · *Sex and Marriage*

The general responsibility of the school for sex education falls outside our scope. This is not an item in the syllabus of a particular subject: it is a task for a particular person, who may be a biologist

---

[1]   For amplification of this theme, see Leslie Weatherhead's *The Trans-forming Friendship.* The life of Helen Keller offers a moving illustration of the creative possibilities of friendship.

or a historian or a domestic science teacher. There are, however, two possibilities before the teacher responsible for religious instruction.

One is to offer an extended course in which the physical facts, the emotional values, the moral imperatives and the Christian insight are integrated. This should probably be arranged outside the timetable provision for religious education, and perhaps before the fourth year. Whether or not this special provision is made, however, there should be a place within the religious discussion for an examination of the Christian attitude to sex and marriage, after the 'facts' are known and assimilated.

We include, in Appendix A, an outline of a course of the first kind which has been offered successfully in a girls' school, described by the teacher responsible. The notes below suggest a way of approach in the normal series of discussions. Here, more than anywhere, teachers will need flexibility and adaptability. Their classes need treatment suitable to their sex, social background, degree of maturity and—that elusive quality—'tone', set so curiously and so markedly by a single individual or small group. The teacher's own personality is a large factor: the young teacher differs in his limitations and opportunities from the old, the single from the married, the secure from the insecure. What is needed above all is sincerity, honesty about the situation in which our young people find themselves, and about the current trend in sexual practices. The Christian persuasion towards high standards is not strengthened by ignoring the powerful pressures towards low ones.

Raising the Problem. Advertisements offer the obvious starting point. They range from the harmless but persistent decorative use of a pretty girl to the scenes heavily loaded with desire. Some proceed on the assumption that a woman's chief aim in life is to catch her man, or that a man should be judged by his success in flirtation. Most of this is not as sinister as is sometimes suggested, but the total pressure towards an interest in sex and a heightening of desire is undeniable. The class may collect such advertisements and examine the assumptions on which they are based; and compare them with the assumptions behind films, novels and television programmes.

Analysis. The desire to find the right man or the right girl is natural and sensible, and the sexual element is of great importance. But will a concentration on it, excluding other elements, really help to find the right person? Is sex-appeal enough? Does a man want a woman for her body alone? What if she is bad-tempered, dishonest, selfish? Does a woman want a partner whose interest will turn to someone else when her physical attraction has faded? Life is longer than a Hollywood romance: will she not need in the years to come a love based on respect, companionship, loyalty, a husband who will stand with her through good fortune or ill, and with her build a home where their children can share that love? The class might write at this stage a short essay on *My Ideal Husband,* or *Wife.*

The Christian Judgement.   Christian teaching on sex is often represented by its critics as an austere self-control arising from a shameful horror of the sex-impulse; but its true purpose is an affirmation of the family. Jesus welcomed and reaffirmed (Mark 7.10; 10.7, 19) the Old Testament teaching on the family, as a close-knit, intimate community in which children could grow in security and learn all they needed for the purposes of life. Father-hood and motherhood were thus of supreme importance, and the sexual drive was to be subordinated to this rich and rewarding duty.

Christians have continued to assert that the family provides an essential means of growth towards the highest type of personality, and have been clear in their warning against letting the sex-impulse take its own way. Chastity before marriage, faithfulness within it, are a means whereby the family itself becomes safe, and both for the children and the parents this security is essential to trust and openness and love. We cannot reconcile the open honesty that husband and wife must have for each other with the furtive concealments and lies that beset an irregular liaison. Jesus showed his acceptance of the family when he rejoiced in a wedding (John 2.1-11), and resisted the idea of divorce (Mark 10.2-12); and Paul reminded parents and children of their duty to each other (Eph. 6.1 ff.)

This is a demanding ideal, that is often not realized, even by committed Christians. In a sick society it may prove a heavy load to bear, and our unscrupulous advertising is a sign of sickness. But within the Christian scheme of values there can be no doubt of its claim upon us. A man who truly loves a woman will wish to bring to her the whole of his love, physical and emotional, unspoilt by early adventures and by later wandering.

Application.   The class may be invited to raise questions, either openly in discussion or on paper through a question box. There is room for honest discussion of difficulties between married people, facing the fact that married life is rarely as smooth as the love-stories imply, and that what matters is not that disagreements arise but the way they are met and the will to resolve them. Or the teacher may outline the findings of the recent studies of delinquency, which trace much of it to some measure of insecurity in the home. Ezekiel's warning (18.2) that 'the fathers have eaten sour grapes, and the children's teeth are set on edge' takes on a new relevance in the present situation.

3 · Snobbery

Raising the Problem.   There should be no difficulty in making a start here. 'Let's have a talk about snobbery' would probably be all that is needed. 'Do you ever have the feeling that people look down on you? Do you ever notice yourself looking down on someone else?'

A more sophisticated approach would be to quote from the American Declaration of Independence: 'We hold these truths to be self-evident, that all men are created equal; that they are endowed by their Creator with inalienable rights ...' This is a statement by the American people of what they believe to be true; and that is why they have no earls and dukes. Could the English people say the same?

Snob appeal is a favourite motive in advertisements; furniture, jewellery, luxury yachts, clothes, used to convey the suggestion that 'top people', who are considered to set the tone of society, smoke a particular cigarette or buy a certain brand of tinned peas.

Analysis.   Discuss the meaning and cause of snobbery, eliciting ideas which may be sharpened up as follows. Snobbery arises from:

the natural tendency to mix more easily with people like ourselves, and to be suspicious and a little afraid of strangers (the in-group and the out-group);

the common desire to 'move up', to mix with people more important than ourselves, and thus to be noticed and envied;

making use of irrelevancies to pass judgement on people, evaluating them by what they have (money, possessions, skill, appearance, accent) instead of what they are.

Face the facts of inequality here: people are not all identical, and nobody wants them to be. Somebody must take decisions, and must be in a position to influence other people. Hence we make use of marks of dignity and status; and important people are made to look important. This point may cause argument, but sufficient concrete instances should dispose of it: school teams, corridor duty, traffic police, producing a play, all demand leadership and the giving of instructions. Prefects wear badges, police wear uniforms, Cabinet Ministers are surrounded by a little pomp that enables them to carry weight.

But the person with a less important job is as human as the one with a more important job. It is in 'being human' that the idea of equality has emerged: whoever we are, we have the same human needs, for food and clothing and shelter, respect and affection, and the same capacity to suffer. We are all important to ourselves.

The problem thus becomes: How can we accept the idea that some people must have more authority than others without implying that they are necessarily more 'valuable'? How can we, personally, learn to avoid being snobbish, and not to mind the snobbery of others? And so arrange society that snobbery will grow less?

The Christian Judgement.   Christians have seen the answer in the idea that all men are equal in the sight of God. But they have had different ways of expressing this idea, ranging from the Catholic teaching on the dignity of certain offices, Pope and King, whose holders perform acts of humility before God (Maundy Thursday), to the Quaker system of lay organization, business meeting without a vote, with everyone free to speak, and worship without clergy, in which everyone may offer a message. By these different means Christians try to assert their belief in an equality of worth. But Christians may fall into the snobbish habits common to us all. They sometimes reveal the tendency to form in-groups, so that a church congregation may seem unfriendly, or the sect may think that it alone is the true church. This is a failure of the Christian ideal. Consider Jesus and the out-groups: Zacchaeus, the Samaritans, Matthew the publican, the woman taken in adultery. Compare Philip and the Ethiopian eunuch, Peter and Paul and the admission of Gentiles.

Christians sometimes join in the game of social climbing, and in the days when church-going was part of the respectable life one church congregation felt and looked 'superior' to another. The class may feel this is still true. Here compare the attitude of Jesus, no 'respecter of persons', choosing his disciples from among ordinary working folk. The earliest disciples from the influential classes, as we should now consider them, were St Paul and St Luke.

Finally, Christians, like others, may fall into the error of judging by externals, particularly moral externals, the conformity to church standards of conduct. But 'The kingdom of heaven is within you . . . Judge not . . . Consider the lilies . . . Blessed are the poor . . .'

Application. Can the Christian ideal be realized? Or is it merely sentiment? If we approach other people thinking more of their humanity (their genuineness, warmth of heart, courage, humour, and their needs for affection and respect) than of their status and importance, we find, as a matter of experience, that we begin to escape from snobbery and the fear of snobbery. If we remember that other people are able to suffer as we are, and that snobbery is often a device to conceal a sense of inferiority, of being hurt, we are more ready to speak to the stranger ('How should I feel in a strange place?') because he is human; less anxious to impress the important, because they too are human; less impressed by externals.

This actually happens, and we can all find out that is happens if we try it. From this experience springs the Christian attack on slavery, poverty, lack of education, disease. Compare the past and present attitudes to lepers and to mental disease (Jesus set about curing them both at a time when other men dreaded them both) to the differences in past and present status of the sexes.

In districts where this is relevant, the colour problem might be raised. With able classes the discussion can proceed to the East-West conflict. What does it mean to say that Russians, English and Americans are equal in the sight of God?

4 · *Money*

Raising the Problem. The issues here are comprehensible enough to be handled in a dialogue, tape-recorded, or rehearsed and presented in front of the class. The following script is a merely suggestive sketch. The children should be asked to devise something fuller, presenting the problem as they see it.

(Noises of traffic in a street.)

Roy	Hiya, Jim, come for a coke.
Jim	Huh. Only if you can lend me a bob.
Roy	Lend you a bob? I thought you were in the money?
Jim	Haven't a bean.
Roy	Why, where's your wages? Been robbed?
Jim	Robbed, aye, that's what it is. Eight flippin' quid a week they said I'd get, and now I haven't a cent.
Roy	Why, who's robbed you?
Jim	Everyone. They never gave me eight quid. There was six notes and some silver in my packet—insurance and income tax they said they'd knocked off. Then the union secretary got at me and swiped five bob. Then there was a quid on the bike, and a bit went on fags. Then my mum took three quid off me for board—three quid, I ask you! And now I haven't a cent. Eight flippin' quid!
Roy	Well, I've got half a dollar left. I'll lend you a bob. Come on.

Analysis. The class may draw up a statement of Jim's account.

IN		s	d	OUT		s	d
Wages	£8	0	0	Board	£3	0	0
Loan		1	0	Insurance		9	11
				Income tax		17	0
				Union		5	0
				Motor cycle	£1	0	0
				A 'bit on fags'	£2	8	1
				Coke		1	0
Total	£8	1	0	*Total*	£8	1	0

Discuss the various items. Jim seemed sore about his mother's charge for board: was it excessive? (Food 30s, leaving 30s for his share of the rent and rates, light, heat, clothes-washing, wear and tear on furniture and equipment). What is national insurance for? Income tax? Union subscription? Is it wise to leave the 'bit on fags' unaccounted for? He will have to buy clothes one day: what else?

He finishes the week a shilling in debt. Would Mr Micawber approve? Could everyone spend like this, to be a shilling in debt? There must be some Roys who can lend.

This first attack is thus on the level of prudence. Common sense in the use of resources is a Christian duty, self-evident, needing no religious appeal, but of serious moment. If we are to give of our strength, we must have the strength. Jim made the mistake of letting things happen to him instead of being responsible about them. The budget is a necessity, claims on us are real claims, and our place in society has to be paid for.

Then turn to Roy, who had a little over to lend to Jim. This may have been good luck or good planning. Ought we to plan to have a little over? Discuss saving for prudence and saving for generosity. Note the 'welfare state' element in income tax and national insurance: the agreed guarantee from all wage-earners to the sick, unemployed or aged. Would we prefer to have the money and risk it? Would we like other people to have to risk it? Try to humanize the impersonal welfare system here, to think of people known to the class who rely on this method of sharing out the nation's resources: the pensioner with no children to support her, the widow with several children, the worker crippled on his job. This aspect of the welfare state emanates from the Christian conscience: in the early days the trade unions were rooted in Christian congregations, as their use of the word 'chapel' serves to remind us.

But does the compulsory, welfare state element meet all problems? Consider some of the good causes, familiar to the children through school collections, that are not publicly provided. Ought we to feel responsible about these, or are they just another thing that happens? Can we arrive at a proportion of our income that we ought to give away?

Finally, attack the common assumption that money will do almost anything (strikes over pay are most common in the motor industry where wages are highest); the pools; changing one's job for a few more shillings a week; the pressure of advertisements—beauty, poise and a boy-friend for 7s 6d a week spent on Dentowash. Will it buy happiness? What makes a person happy? Will it buy love and friendship? Do people like us for what we have or for what we are? Will it buy courage?—millionaires are occupationally prone to suicide. Compare 'The love of money is the root of all evil' (Timothy 6.10) with Gert and Daisy's 'They say money's the root of all evil, but my, aint it good for the nerves!' Is there any real conflict here? The *love* and the *prudent* use are very different things.

The Christian Judgement. The teaching of Jesus is concerned not with money but with motive. Money is one among many means of generous human relationships and the worship of God. The widow's mite (Mark 12.41-4), the good Samaritan (Luke 10.35-37), the prodigal son (Luke 15.11-24) convey a spirit of concern for persons and their needs in which money becomes a means of giving. It is never the only means; and the word 'charity' has lost much of its original loveliness because of those who thought they had done all that was necessary when they subscribed to an appeal for funds. In this larger context, prudence and foresight are still necessary, but are directed not towards security but towards the power to give. See Luke 6.38 for the spirit of Christian giving— 'good measure, pressed down and shaken together'.

Application. Draw up a budget for Jim, providing for sensible spending on himself and what will make him happy; on duties to other people; and leaving a margin for spontaneous generosity. The Christian judgement may be applied to the ethics of a strike; and to the contrast between the standard of living in the East and in the West.

5 · Work

Raising the Problem. Collect some advertisements that appeal to the labour-saving incentive (the husband with his feet up saying, 'I'm doing the washing'; 'Takes the drudgery out of washing day'; 'A wipe—a rub—and it's clean'). Collect information about gadgets in the children's homes, and discuss how much time they save. Do we welcome these things? Most certainly, though some are not very efficient, and some rob work of its delight. But is the idea behind the advertisements, that work is only to be 'saved' or 'dodged', a sound one?

Analysis. Men have often thought so. The writer of Genesis thought so, for he regarded man's work and woman's childbearing as punishment for the sin of Adam and Eve; and many in modern industry think so, as they agitate for shorter hours and bigger pay, or, as some workers do, as they spin out a job so that overtime has to be worked to finish it. Teachers who do not know what the fathers of their class work at should pick their way carefully here.

Is this the general view? Do some people *like* work? Are they the 'mugs'? Or are they merely lucky in having an interesting job? We need to be honest here: many jobs are dull all the time, most are dull some of the time. What does the class think about work after its experience of school life? Even so, would it like to do nothing all day? After a certain amount of loose talk on this issue, hold them down to a few of the hard facts of work.

Work has to be done. Man has to live. Growing food and making clothes and shelter, bringing up children and maintaining the home are basic necessities. But if men really believed that work was evil, they would have stopped at this level, cut this labour to the minimum, and spent the rest of the time in idleness.

Men can turn their necessities into pleasures. We need to eat, but we do not *need* to cook exciting food, yet people do. And much of the world's work is not necessary, but contributes to the happiness and interest of life: the journalist, the entertainer, the professional footballer, the maker of motor-cars, the designer of wallpapers. This suggests the need for finding out what goes on in an industry we think of entering, and wondering if, on the whole, we should enjoy doing *that,* and should be rewarded by the sense that it was in some way important. The pay matters, but the difference of a few shillings a week, spent on half an hour's pleasure, is of less importance than the difference between interest and boredom for seven or eight hours a day.

In modern conditions work is often of little intrinsic importance to the worker himself. The car-factory worker does not take his work home, or see it through to the finished product. The importance of the work thus lies in its importance to other people. This aspect of it is central: it is service rendered; it is what we give to the common life.

The Christian Judgement. There are references in the Bible to some of the common sense of work. *Proverbs* warns us against shirking (6.6-11; 15.19; 26.14-16). The New Testament assumes obedience to this imperative, and turns, as all the teaching of Jesus turns, to the motive of all living, which would transform our attitude to work as it does our attitude to everything else. 'Loving our neighbour' includes faithful service in all our relations with him. When those for whom we work strike us as unsatisfactory, we are held by the command: 'With good will doing service, as to the Lord and not to men' (Eph 6.7). Discuss what this means, in everyday terms: 'with a good will', instead of reluctantly; 'as to the Lord', working as if the Lord were to see it; 'and not to men', not doing only what you are strictly paid for or seen to be doing.

Application. The application of these ideas to the industrial situation at large would probably be difficult. An intelligent class might break into two groups to draw up a 'Managers' Charter' and a

'Workmen's Charter', not making demands on the other side, which charters usually do, but each side pledging what it had to give: a Christian rule of work made by managers as an ideal for managers, and workers for workers. A simpler approach would be to ask for stories of the difficulties their friends may have found themselves in when they began to work; and to enlarge these with reference to the situations that sometimes figure in the papers: workers sent to Coventry for working too hard, a pit accident that occurred because someone had neglected his maintenance work, or had deserted his observation post for a smoke.

6 · *Leisure*

Raising the Problem.   The class may be asked if they ever have arguments with their parents over the way they spend their evenings and holidays; or, if a less direct approach is needed, they may work out a brief conversation between parents and child, about what they do when they are out of the house. The 'parents' should bring out their feeling that the young ought to spend some of their evenings at home, doing something useful, and the child's feeling that 'his time's his own'.

Analysis.   Discuss the points raised, and bring out the distinction between compulsory activity (work, sleep, meals) and 'free' time, that we may dispose of according to our personal choice. But what does 'free' mean? Not free to do harm; nor, surely, free to do nothing; free, rather, to be ourselves, to do the things that are characteristic of us, instead of being imposed by somebody else.

What does 'being ourselves' mean? Discuss the way leisure pursuits can provide for interests and activity impossible in work. Canned entertainment is clearly legitimate, restful, and to some extent re-creative ('It takes me out of myself'), but in the end unsatisfying; and many young people find it so. Lead on to the need at some point and in some degree to *do* things. We are most ourselves in action.

The problem then becomes: 'How can we plan our leisure time so as to be ourselves most completely, with a suitable mixture of rest and passive entertainment with action?'

The Christian Judgement.   The Bible has nothing of importance to say directly about leisure, for in biblical times there was not enough leisure to present a problem. We may consider the teaching on the Sabbath, a day when work was reduced to a minimum in order that men should look to the whole meaning of life, and worship God from whom life came; the danger of observing the rules about the Sabbath while missing its essential meaning; and the use Jesus made of this to point his teaching, that right conduct springs from pure motive. The Sabbath is 'made for man' to express his true nature as a worshipping being, and not to be either enslaved by work or made gloomy by prohibitions. What is true of the Sabbath is true of all leisure, given to us for our growth as persons, not to be frittered away: 'Whatsoever things are true, whatsoever things are honest, whatsoever things are just, whatsoever things are pure, whatsoever things are lovely, whatsoever things are of good report; if there be any virtue, if there be any praise, think on these things.'

Application.   The class might consider the way these principles work out on a large scale: delinquency and the street gang, where idleness is an opportunity for 'looking for trouble'; the demand for canned entertainment, legitimate in itself, but creating huge industries with a dangerous power to shape our thought and moral standards.

7 · *Prayer*

Raising the Problem.   This may be raised directly: 'One of the things Christians are taught to do is to pray. What do you think they mean by prayer?' This should provoke some definitions and difficulties: asking God to help you, asking for things you want, asking God to help other people, to make them better when they are ill; but it doesn't work. The teacher can then raise the problems discussed below, if he finds the class uncritical; or analyse their difficulties if they are provocative enough.

Analysis.   It is the *duty* of the teacher to raise the root problem: that praying seems to be 'pushing God around', telling him what to do, suggesting good ideas he had not thought of for himself, trying to manipulate the laws of the universe with our own thoughts. If children are allowed to go out into the world with this infantile view of prayer, we have let them down. If they keep it, as some do, they will be fixed there for the rest of their lives, at an immature religious response. If, as is more likely, they grow out of it instead of growing through it, they may give up all their spiritual quest at the same time. Press them, then, with the question: 'What do you think *happens* when you ask God for something?' They may try to 'solve' the problem empirically on two or three instances ('I prayed for my grandmother but she died . . . I prayed for fine weather and it came'). But is should not be difficult to demonstrate that this is a very chancy way of conducting one's life. Teachers with any knowledge of magic may draw analogies.

A mature form could easily be led to see that a belief in this kind of prayer implies a curious belief in God: that he is a being of uncertain temper, who will not do the right things unless somebody asks him; that he is forgetful, and needs reminding; or that he works like a slot-machine.

Christian Teaching.   Prayer is central to all the world's religions, but Christian prayer is different from all others, because it springs from the Christian view of God as Father. Christian teaching about prayer arises first from the teaching and example of Jesus. Examine first the Lord's Prayer, then the two accounts of Jesus himself at prayer, the Temptations and the scene in the garden.

The Lord's Prayer is not to be thought of as a 'piece' to be said in chorus, but as a framework of meditation and commitment. A word first, then, on what we actually *do* when we pray: we shut out all distractions and try to concentrate our mind on the truth about life, the deepest truth, beneath our ordinary comings and goings, idle thoughts and desires. When we are faced by a bewildering personal problem, a quarrel, a difficult choice, we sometimes go out for a walk by ourselves to 'see things straight'. When we pray we are trying to see life straight.

Our Father, which art in heaven.   So prayer begins in an effort to hold our minds to the belief that God is good, and that he is 'in heaven'—not 'above the sky', away from it all, but unshaken by what shakes us. He is safe, unchanging, and the universe, infinitely greater than our own concerns, is in his hands. To start praying is thus to put ourselves in a large place, in which our affairs are cut to life-size, instead of being, as they so often seem to us, larger than life.

Thy kingdom come, thy will be done.   Here we put ourselves in line with God's intention for the world, joining with him in the will to good and right. We do not mean to say to God, 'You do it: I give up' but 'You are at work to get it right; I am with you.'

Give us this day our daily bread. God *does* this. Man digs and tends, but he does not make his food. This is part of the idea of God, the mysterious power by which we live, and without which we could not survive. Imagine what would happen if all moisture were suddenly withdrawn from the world: the taps dry, the grass withering, the human body collapsing into dust—a science fiction theme that no writer has dared to imagine. In praying for our daily bread we say 'Give' meaning: 'I know where my bread comes from; you are at work in the process; I am with you.'

Forgive us our sins, as we forgive them that sin against us. 'Sins' rather than 'trespasses' or 'debts' here, for trespass and debt both have narrow connotations, particularly for the schoolboy. This is the simplest clause in the prayer. The adolescent is aware of guilt and involved in quarrels. Archbishop Temple used to say that he often asked schoolboys at what point they began to mean business when they said the Lord's Prayer: and they answered, 'Forgive us our sins.' Clearness of conscience before God is tied up with clearness with other human beings. A family is not united if two members are at loggerheads, and two sons are not clear with their father if they are quarrelling. So we here repeat, from our side, the two great commandments: 'Thou shalt love the Lord thy God ... and thy neighbour as thyself.' We say, 'I know that you are at work in the world, towards love and unity; and I am with you.'

Lead us not into temptation, but deliver us from evil. If thought of as a simple petition, this is the most difficult clause. It must be viewed more as assertion and affirmation: God does not lead us into temptation. He does not, deliberately, try us out. He is not that sort of God. But 'trial', in the sense of difficulty to be overcome, problems to be solved, is the human condition. Mature Christians reach a point where they welcome difficulty as an opportunity. We all welcome opportunities to show what we are made of, as an Olympic high-jumper would be sadly disappointed if he were never allowed to try anything over five feet. And though this is rarely applicable to genuine suffering, to the trial that takes us to breaking point, when such trials come the Christian response is not, 'Why have you done this to me?' but 'I know you are at work, seeking with me the highest answer to this situation: you *are* delivering me from this evil; you are giving me the strength to bear it; and I am with you.'

For thine is the kingdom. This is plain assertion and commitment. We are not, at root, asking God to help us with *our* concerns: we are offering ourselves to help with his. The universe he made is the scene of a conflict between good and evil. Good and truth are mighty, and will prevail. We are with him.

In the light of this study, consider the story of the Temptations and of the solitude in Gethsemane. In the first, Jesus was making his choice of the way he should do his work for mankind: by economic reform, by political action, or by such display of power as would win men's allegiance to himself. He chose to go forward in simple dependence on the will of God. In Gethsemane, all the powers he had rejected hurled themselves on his own head: greed, political machination, and the status-anxiety of the Jews. He shrank from this apparent catastrophe, but 'nevertheless not my will but thine.' There is no trace here of magic, or the desire to manipulate the universe: only the prayer of commitment and dependence.

There is much more to be said about prayer, and some classes will want to know *how* to pray. But the root problem is to convey a mature view of prayer. The classroom is not the ideal place for devotional instruction, which many will find irrelevant and embarrassing, but for clarifying concepts. It will be seen that the teaching of Jesus about prayer does not involve the problem of 'pushing God around', for it does not ask God to suspend the laws of nature, but to sustain them. Prayer 'works', therefore, by opening to God an opportunity of enlisting our resources, not by asking him to change his intention in order to support ours.

Application.   The whole subject is so personal that the concluding stage should probably be confined to the examination of situations in which prayer illuminates, sustains and empowers, to the moral and spiritual discrimination it confers. There is a strong case, however, for moving at this point to a consideration of the worship of the Church. The difficulty here is the variety of concepts (symbolic ritual, hearty singing, emotional crisis, sacramental silence—they will all be there). To the child the worship of the Church means what he does himself, or has given up doing, on Sunday. The teacher needs to know his class and their backgrounds well before he can cut a way through this. If he does, there is scope for a candid exchange on the forms of worship with which they are familiar, what is done and why. They will soon find they do not know, and the teacher may enlist the help of local clergy, either in person, or by getting a few children to interview them and bring back reports. The tape-recorder and the 'face-to-face' interviewing technique may be helpful here.

One practical issue is worth raising, by applying the test we often apply to moral actions: What would happen if everybody did it? What sort of world would it be if everyone tried to travel on trains without a ticket? got drunk? did as little and as dishonest work as possible? Similarly, what kind of world might it become if everyone started the day with ten minutes of quiet listening for truth, resolve to stand by the truth, trust in the power of love? Suppose people *really* did this—politicians, journalists, advertisers, salesmen, managers, professional entertainers?

8 · *Suffering*

Raising the problem. In dealing with suffering, it is essential first to establish the level at which it would be faced. The death of an elderly relative ('Our gran died last week, and our mum was ever so upset') cannot really be said to pose the problem, although it may be the only contact some of the children have with suffering. The class may be asked beforehand to bring newspaper cuttings of all kinds of suffering—accidents on the road, disasters at sea, in the air, in mines, murder and violence, disease, refugees. After the analysis these could be classified, and posted in a wall news-paper as the discussions proceed.

Analysis. A clear analysis removes part of the difficulty. An approach through road accidents would reveal the main points. They are caused by:

(a) *Speed.* Men want to go fast, but they live too close together to go fast with complete safety. There is no escape from this except either by agreeing that nobody goes fast or by not having so many people. Some measure of control of this problem is possible to men, if we could decide that speed was less important than life.

(b) *Carelessness.* The occasional misjudgement or wandering of attention is also in man's power to control, but he does not make the effort.

(c) *Sinful carelessness:* drink, selfishness, competitiveness, and bad workmanship in the factory or repair-shop.

(d) *Fog, ice, floods, landslips.* Some human error, ignorance, lack of skill may enter here: Was the fog forecast? Did the driver find out about road conditions before he started? Did he over-estimate his own skill? But there is also an element of natural hazard over which he has no control.

These factors may be generalized as:

(a) the desire to do things which are known to be dangerous in the conditions of life as we know them;
(b) carelessness, ignorance, lack of skill;
(c) sinfulness, greed, selfishness;
(d) defeat by the forces of nature.

The first three categories are aspects of human error, and do not raise the true problem of suffering. This is a real world, in which a real offence against its laws brings real consequences. We must not grumble because we take risks. If we do not want to 'play safe' all our lives—and we do not—then we must 'play dangerously'. But the danger we play with is a real danger.

This leaves still the question of 'fairness'. The drunken driver often kills somebody else. But this is also a part of the condition of life. We live together, we need to live together, and we like living together. We depend on each other. And it is not a real dependence unless we can let each other down. If we could help each other but not hurt each other life would be make-believe.

This fourfold analysis may be applied to disease:

(a) Lung cancer and heart troubles that arise from foolish habits.
(b) Tetanus, sepsis, that arise from carelessness and ignorance.
(c) Alcoholism, V.D., some mental disturbances that arise from sin.
(d) Epidemics that we cannot control.

This is a rough classification, which is open to objection; but as far as it goes it opens up the distinction between what we can easily explain and what we cannot explain.

Even suffering that can be 'explained', in the sense that a cause may be found in man's ignorance or evil will, still has to be borne; and it is here that we need the Christian insight.

Christian Teaching. We must beware of giving the impression that 'Christianity' offers a slick answer to the problem of suffering. What the Christian discovers is ground to stand on in the mystery. Christianity is not primarily a way of 'explaining' the world: it is a way of living in it.

The class may consider the following passages:

(a) Luke 10.30-37. The Christian seeks to relieve the suffering of others. Consider what the victim would have had to say about suffering before and after the arrival of the good Samaritan. Before, he would have been obsessed by the unfairness of it all; after he would have been most of all grateful for a goodness that *without the suffering* he would never have known. This does not explain or justify the suffering, but it makes it mean something new.

(b) Mark 15.15-39. Jesus experienced suffering at a peculiarly agonizing level: the sheer physical pain, the utter isolation, the betrayal, the complete injustice of it. He triumphed over it by feeling no bitterness: he sealed off the evil, so that his followers, instead of seeking revenge, which would have extended the evil, set out with love and a message of love. The suffering caused by human evil the Christian seeks to meet with love, to prevent its repetition and extension by accepting it in the spirit Jesus showed: the 'fellowship of his sufferings' (Phil. 3.10; 1 Peter 4.12-13).

(c) Mark 7.37. Revelation 7.9-17; Romans 8.28. To the Christian suffering is evil, but not *unmitigated* evil for it is mitigated by Christian love, drawing people together out of their isolation, and by the belief that this life is not all the story. We do not know what happens outside this time-sequence, after death; but we believe that in the end the universe is in the hand of God.

Application. The most positive line to follow here would be the consideration of the forms of large-scale suffering in the world: refugees, poverty, the consequences of crime. How may they be met? How can their causes be removed? How can the sufferers be reached and strengthened? Consider the relatively recent progress made in this country in dealing with bedrock poverty; and discuss the responsibility of wealthy nations towards poorer ones. Consider also war as a cause of suffering. How may war be avoided? The class will not know, their teachers do not know, and the Church is not agreed. The Christian is not omniscient: he is concerned; and if we can arouse our school leavers to concern we have set them in the right direction.

9 · *Death*

Raising the Problem. Beware of raising this problem in too concrete a form, such as the death of a schoolmate or a local tragedy. We can afford to generalize here, because everyone is aware that he himself will die, so the generalization is based on a fact of experience, and enables the private anxiety to be dealt with in a general and manageable form. One approach is to issue sheets of paper and ask the class to write five to ten lines on each of two questions:

1 What do you think is the Christian belief about life after death?
2 What do you think yourself?

The first question should produce angels, harps and golden crowns and the rest, as well as some more mature statements. The second should offer a variety, ranging from 'nothing' to spiritualism and reincarnation. Collect these and before the next lesson analyse them into groups. Form a brains trust of intelligent representatives of each group in the answers to the second question, leaving the first for the examination of Christian teaching. Let each member of the brains trust offer a brief account of his point of view, and then defend himself against the others and the class.

Analysis. The analysis should emerge from the discussion. The teacher may either intervene or sum up at the end, with the following points.

(a) There is a great variety of belief here, but this does not mean there is no point in thinking about it. The variety is matched in the world at large. Philosophers such as Socrates, followers of non-Christian religions, non-Christian poets, some eminent modern scientists have been convinced that there is some kind of life after death. What the variety does mean is that there is a great deal of unproved guesswork; as there was about the western hemisphere before Columbus discovered it—but there *was* a western hemisphere.

(b) These detailed guesses cannot be proved or disproved. We do not know what will happen tomorrow: if we did life would be entirely changed. There would be no football pools, no working for examinations, because those who knew they would pass and those who knew they would fail would both give up working; there would be no going on holiday to places where it would rain, no children born if the parents knew the first one would die. It is worth while bringing this out, in view of the bogus astrology going the rounds. If the astrologers were right they would shatter life as we know it. Our present existence relies on not knowing the future in detail.

(c) But to say 'I believe in some sort of future life' means 'I believe that this life really matters'; to say 'I do not believe in a future life of any kind' means 'I do not believe that this life really matters'. And in general, most people have a deep conviction that life really matters. They are against murder and suicide, though they may feel the deepest pity for anyone so miserable that he cannot bear to live any longer. It is this conviction that makes them continue to speculate about a future life. But the detailed guesses cannot be proved or disproved: they can only be graded on the value of their results, in terms of their effect on our attitudes to this life. Thus reincarnation cannot be disproved; but it is open to the objection that it makes *this* life of less importance because it gives us further chances. We do not need to listen to a history lesson if we know we shall get the same thing tomorrow. And our conviction is that this life does matter, in a once-for-all kind of way.

Christian Teaching. Turn now to some of the varieties of view that emerged in the paragraphs on the Christian teaching about the future life, and consider the following references.

Matthew 22.23-33. Jesus swept aside all crude notions about the life after death. We are not to think of this life 'going on' in the same way. That kind of speculation is all beside the point. This enables us to deal with most of the difficulties about 'boredom' in heaven. Tinsel imagery, used by Christians in the middle ages, and still often surviving, has been used as a kind of poetry, as many people talk of retiring to 'a little cottage with roses round the door', though in fact they will settle for a bungalow on a suburban housing estate.

Romans 8.35-9. God's purposes are not defeated by the evil in the world, even by death. 'In the end' God triumphs, and men who know him and respond to him share in the triumph. If we really believe in God, we believe in this: there is no escape from it.

John 17.3. The New Testament is not so much concerned with a future life as with eternal life: the life that matters, the life of value. And we live this life as we respond *now* to God: it begins here. The object of the Church, said Coleridge, is 'another world, not a world to *come* exclusively, but likewise *another that now is.*' The root of the answer to the problem of death is that life matters: our life matters to God, and in some way will continue to matter.

There is much that we cannot hope to know, but as Bishop Lightfoot wrote a week before his death, 'I find that my faith suffers nothing by leaving a thousand questions open, so long as I am convinced on two or three main lines.'

Application.   The argument outlined above may be applied to the narrative of the resurrection of Jesus. Examine the evidence, and be content with doubt among the class as to exactly what happened, 'how' it was done. Compare the statement in Matthew 22. But it is clear that the disciples were convinced that God was not defeated by evil; and that they themselves found a way of life that changed their outlook, released their powers, and sent them travelling up and down the world under the power of a new spirit.

Today the urgency of the belief in eternal life and resurrection lies not in 'What is it like?' or in 'Who moved the stone?' but in 'What are eternal values?' and 'How can men be moved to respond to them?' How can they be made to *tingle* with excitement about the things that matter, with the sense of urgency, of a choice between infinite loss and infinite gain? The Christian proclamation of eternal life is an assertion of the eternal Now, the ultimate value of the immediate.

10 · *Learning*

Raising the Problem.   Since this is very close to their present condition, they will respond to a direct attack. 'Are you looking forward to leaving school? Why?' Among the answers will appear, or can be made to appear, the 'boredom' and difficulty of lessons. Nevertheless, have you learnt anything at school that will be of value to you later? Discuss the school curriculum from this point of view, and elicit the idea that much of this knowledge and skill is useful because it tells us about the world we live in, the people who live in it with us, and how to live in it successfully—language and number, science, geography, literature, cookery, crafts. This turns on the question: '*How?* How does the world live? How can I get on in it?' But such useful knowledge does not answer the question: 'Why?' Why is the world there? Why must I live? What is it all for? Any guesses or attempts to answer these questions will be found to lean heavily on what has been learnt outside school, from parents, church or friends.

Analysis.   Here we come to the most difficult moment of the whole series of discussions. It may be thought too difficult to attempt, but to avoid it is to declare a belief that these pupils are, at root, 'ineducable'. For here is the basic concept of eduction: the idea that man can escape from his material environment by the use of abstraction, the belief that man can learn to think about his condition. It would probably pay to begin this stage with a warning that it is going to be difficult, that it will 'hurt', just as climbing a mountain hurts. But we climb a mountain to get a view; and so with this mountain. The argument runs on these lines:

(a) *Knowledge, information and belief.* In our understanding of anything, a table or a piano, a pet or a friend, there are some things we really know for ourselves, and some things we are told by others, and some things we do not 'know' at all. Discuss what we know about a desk. We know for ourselves something about its shape, colour, hardness. We are told that it is made of wood, which has a certain chemistry; we are told how it is made, and what it is for. There remain some things we do not know: whether it will collapse, and whether it is still there when nobody is looking at it. These three levels of knowledge may be labelled, for convenience, fact, information and belief.

Apply this method to a person, and notice that what we know as fact is curiously little and unimportant compared with what we do not know. Notice that in all our actions we have to make use of all three kinds of understanding: to use a desk properly we need to know the fact of it, the feel of it; to know what it is for; and to believe that it will still be there when we stop looking at it. In dealing with persons we must see them, rely on information they give us about themselves, and believe that they are not rogues trying to deceive us. Sometimes they are, and then our belief has let us down; but if we start out believing that everyone is a rogue, then *that* belief will let us down too, and more frequently.

This analysis should be extended as long as is necessary to reach the point where the class see that 'belief', in the sense of acting on what is not known for 'certain', enters into all our experience.

(b) *Proof.* The philosopher or the scientist has rigorous methods of proof which most of us do not use in ordinary life. For our normal purposes to prove anything is to present a statement in such a way that an intelligent person can accept it. We have no need to prove fact: we know it for ourselves. Information may be proved in two ways: first by demonstrating it as fact ('Water never gets hotter than 100 degrees centigrade', proved by boiling some with a thermometer in it); second by an argument so clear and logical that it cannot be shaken. This last is the philosopher's, and often the scientist's, proof. What we 'know' about the inside of the atom is the result of argument.

The class may here look back over their school learning, and collect instances of different kinds of proof they have made use of: experiments in science, how we know history happened, how we build up a picture of a character in a book, how we could prove it will rain on the southern slopes of the Himalayas next July, practical and theoretical geometry.

But much information we accept without either of these kinds of proof, simply because we have not time to make the necessary tests. Much school information, such as the climate of the monsoon lands, or the fact that cars are exports of Great Britain, we accept on authority because we know we could test it for ourselves if we had sufficient time. Theories in science we could, perhaps, work out if we were clever enough. We accept this kind of information because we believe that the people who inform us are honest and reliable. Sometimes they are not, but the same argument applies as above: if we believed everyone a liar all the time we should be worse off than we are.

The third level, that we call belief, cannot be 'proved' at all, in the sense of being demonstrated; yet we must 'believe' whenever we decide to act. We never know for certain all the facts involved in an action. How can we decide whether one belief is better than another? The class may choose here between two beliefs about strangers, as a guide to action:

1 Strangers are likely to be unfriendly.
2 Strangers are likely to be friendly.

If we choose the first, we shall probably also decide to be unfriendly to them. But then we shall never find out whether they meant to be friendly or not, for they will respond with enmity to our enmity. If we choose the second, we shall be more willing to be friendly to them. Then we shall find out about them; and even if we were wrong, and they are in fact unfriendly, we at least know the answer.

Compare, similarly,

1   Tennis is a silly game.
2   Tennis is a good game.

If we choose the first, we shall not trouble to learn tennis, and shall never know whether we were right or wrong. If we choose the second, we shall learn it, and shall know whether it is 'silly' or not. This method may be generalized into the statement that a 'good' belief is one that opens us out to experience, challenges us to action, sets us on the move. The opponents of slavery thus held a belief that was impossible to prove from the facts of the time; but is was a good belief—that though slaves looked inferior to their white masters, they were not inferior—that opened up the situation, set the liberators working, and in the end demonstrated that slaves were not truly inferior to whites.

Other instances of a 'belief' that worked may be examined: the status of women, who, it was believed, were inferior to men; but now they show themselves equally capable in any direction except the physical; or the 'poor', who were once thought incapable of education.

There is a great deal more to be said about belief, but this point will serve our purpose. Good teaching always relies on learning the minimum required for progress.

Christian Teaching.   The class should now be in a position to apply this analysis to what they have learnt about Christianity.

(a)   *Fact.*   They have little pure fact to deal with here, unless they have undergone a conversion experience. A church may be able to handle such experiences, but they are difficult to deal with in school. The existence and work of the church, the character of Christians, may be known as first-hand facts, but the experience of some children may be unhappy here. This lack of fact, however, is not an argument against a religious belief. If we do not 'know' that God created the world, we equally certainly do not 'know' that he did not.

(b)   *Information.*   The Bible, religious history and biography, and religious argument and persuasion rest on information. Some of it can be supported by convincing evidence: archaeology and history bring out, what many schoolchildren do not realize, that a great deal of the work of scholars supports our belief in the historicity of the Bible. But the teacher needs to recognize that 'information' can be carried about without its affecting belief. The relevance of the biblical world picture to the child's own private world must be established with the kind of vividness that is exercised by a 'fact'.

(c) *Belief.* The class may put together the bare bones of the Christian faith: that there is a God, who created the world for a good end; that Jesus lived a life of such a quality that those who knew him began to say: This is what God is like; that other men are not as complete as he was, quarrel with each other and are at odds with themselves, but find in the life of Jesus an inspiration to grow more complete, and recognize here a power that supports them, befriends them, whom they call the Holy Spirit. Then subject these propositions to the analysis above. 'I believe in God' means 'I believe that the world has a meaning, that it is intended, and therefore I believe in the Intender.' This is a more challenging, valuable, encouraging belief than 'I believe the world has no meaning, was not intended, and is all the result of blind force.'

A class with some academic habit of mind may take to an account of the four classic 'proofs' of the existence of God, none of which we accept as proof in the scientist's or philosopher's sense, but which all correspond to ways in which sensible men find themselves thinking.

1   *The argument from cause* (cosmological).   Science is the study of cause and effect; when we get back to the earliest cause we can discover, we ask, 'What caused that?' This First Cause we call God.

2   *The argument from design* (teleological).   Science reveals an amazing order in the universe, which seems to imply a design. The designer we call God.

3   *The argument from man* (anthropological).   Men feel a need to believe in something higher than themselves. That 'something higher' we call God.

4   *The argument from existence* (ontological).   Man can think of perfect beauty, perfect goodness, absolute power, though these do not come into his experience. That 'absolute' we call God.

These are persuasions rather than proofs. A good class may be able to range them in order of persuasiveness.

We may then move on to the idea of a 'good' God: the proposition that the intention of the universe is towards good. Discuss what content they give to the word 'good', and contrast with evil. What difference would it make to our life if we thought that *in the end* evil would come out on top?

Since for many children God and Jesus seem too remote from the contemporary world to have much influence on everyday life, the concept of the divinity of Christ is best approached from the human end, with the help, for example, of such a book as T. R. Glover's *Jesus of History*. Jesus' friends knew him first as a brave, wise, alert man with a forceful personality and a quick sympathy who had the secret of how to live a full life. When they were with him they found it easier to be the kind of men they wished to become, and were willing to accept him as their leader (John 6.68). Jesus, then, may be viewed as 'the intention for humanity': he was the sort of person that human beings are meant to become. Would not this be more hopeful, a more challenging belief than the belief, say, that all men were meant to be like Napoleon or Hitler, or even that amiable adolescent hero, Cliff Richard?

The teacher ought to go on from here to point out that, while this was where the disciples started, it is not the whole truth about what Christians came to believe about Jesus. Even during his earthly life those who knew him best found it difficult to think of Jesus as an 'ordinary man'. From the start there was something mysterious about him. The gospels show the disciples and others as frequently 'amazed' or 'astonished' and failing to understand. [2]

In common with their fellow-Jews the disciples believed that God was active in the affairs of men, especially in the history of their own nation, and that he had spoken to men through the prophets. But the revelation through the prophets had been fragmentary. Each prophet had expressed only a *part* of the truth about God. But the Old Testament itself points forward to a time when God would reveal himself fully.

Now, after the Resurrection the disciples were conscious of a new power at work in their lives and in the life of the Church (Acts 2). This power, the power of the Holy Spirit, they associated with the risen Lord. As they pondered, in the light of what the prophets had said, on all that Jesus had said and done, they were forced to the conclusion that in him God had acted in a special way, that in him the partial revelation of the Old Testament had been fulfilled. In the end, the only way they could express this was by saying that Jesus is the Son of God; that if you look at Jesus you see exactly what God is like (Hebrews 1.1-3).

2   See, for example, Mark 4.41; 6.45-52; 9.2-8, 15; 10.32; 16.8. And for a fuller treatment of this idea, R. H. Lightfoot's *The Gospel Message of St Mark* (Oxford, 1950), chapter 7.

The doctrine of the Holy Spirit should be linked closely with this note of the hopefulness of the doctrine about Jesus. When men have stood by their belief in God and Christ they have found themselves lifted up, renewed, full of power. Illustrate from Pentecost, the lives of the saints, and religious biography.

From this we can lead on to the necessity for commitment in order to find out. We 'believe' that tennis is worth playing; we learn to play it; and we find it is. We 'believe' that this Christian view of life is worth standing by; we stand by it; and it is. But if we believe in tennis but do nothing about it, tennis remains valueless. This does not matter much, because there are other ways of amusing ourselves. If we believe in the Christian way of life, but do nothing about it, then that too remains valueless. But this does matter, because there is only one life.

Reincarnation may be raised here, though there is no reason for the teacher to raise it. Strictly speaking, it is an irrelevant idea, and since the evidence for it is not susceptible of logical examination, and the theory throws no light on the moral situation of the present life, it has no challenge in itself.

Application. The consequences of believing in a God who loves, who has shown what man is meant to be, and who releases power to men to begin to realize it, are so comprehensive that the discussion can start anywhere. What would happen if people *really* believed this, and acted on it? Warlike dictators, child-kidnappers, tough business men, hooligans, quarrelling married couples, people who 'couldn't care less'? Bring out the issues of responsibility, to each other, to truth, to God; human nature, its present imperfection and its potentiality; and hope in the Spirit.

If this very difficult argument is to make any impact, it must be presented on a basis of 'What happens if . . .?'; not 'This is so.' The Christian may legitimately say: 'This is so for me because I have found it so;' but the school leaver can be reached in his condition only by what he can see for himself. 'What happens if . . .?' is forward-looking and challenging. 'This is so' will be left behind when he leaves us behind and meets those who say it is not so.

CHAPTER SIX

THE PROBLEM METHOD

To speak of a 'problem syllabus' and 'problem method' may seem something of a contradiction in terms. The problem syllabus is as wide-ranging and chaotic as life itself: the problem method appears a hazardous plunge into an ocean of idle chat.

In a sense the charge is true, and is to be welcomed. The syllabus is, to borrow the modern jargon, Anti-syllabus, the method Anti-method. But real life is anti-syllabus. When we have done our best to bind it in categories, it shakes itself and bursts out of them. And if we are to offer our leavers the last piece of preparation for life that they need, we must offer them the power to deal with the shakings and burstings. The syllabus we have sketched must therefore be thought of, in the Quaker phrase, 'not as a rule or form to walk by', but as an illustration of the way in which an individual anti-syllabus may be constructed. Our classes are now aware that they are entering on a bewildering time: we must discover what bewilders them, and face it, not as authorities who have all the answers, but as friends who stand by them as they grapple with their problems.

The same is true of method. 'I feel so strongly,' wrote a headmistress to us, 'that it is well-nigh impossible to lay down any kind of "best approach". I often prepare in detail my approach, and on entering the classroom and sensing the particular situation or atmosphere scrap the whole approach and attack it from another angle entirely.' It would be a fatal mistake to go into class determined that come what may the discussion will follow predetermined lines, that all the correct points will be made, and that orthodox conclusions will be reached. Mathematical problems must be solved correctly, but life is not mathematics, and we are dealing here with life.

This does not mean that the teacher can go in to class saying, 'Well, now, let us have a discussion. What would you like to discuss?' The headmistress we have quoted says, 'I prepare my approach and sometimes scrap it.' We must have an approach prepared; we must be ready to scrap it; but we must always have something to scrap. Extempore lessons may sometimes be the best teaching, but we must extemporize on a theme; and we shall not feel safe to extemporize unless there is a prepared approach to fall back on if the spark does not come.

To this extent 'method' is a matter of plain sense. But there is a deeper level of justification. The boys and girls must learn that thought and discussion are as methodical as any other means of learning, that problems in religion and morals can be approached as methodically as problems in any other field. We are concerned in religious education, as in all education, with how to think. The Christian does not, or should not, think in a different way from other people, though the dimensions in which he operates give him more to think about.

It is to this end that we have set out the four stages of a discussion. Rarely will the movement from one stage to another be clearly marked. Often the teacher will begin with the Christian teaching, as a sure means of provoking his sceptics into argument. Sometimes he may start with the 'application', when, for example, a newspaper report raises such a question as 'Ought Christians to be against the Bomb?' What matters is not that the discussion should move in a particular way, but that the members of the class should establish the habit of asking, over anything they are arguing about: 'What is the problem?' 'What is the Christian teaching about it?' and 'What would happen if that teaching were genuinely accepted and put into practice?'

Indeed many teachers could achieve the situation we have described without departing from their usual methods of instruction, reading, perhaps, a passage from the Bible and chatting about its relevance to human life, so long as they maintain a relaxed, friendly atmosphere in the classroom, and are seen to be open and honest, undogmatic and accessible to another point of view. Many teachers, however, will need to take a deliberate step out of the old teacher-pupil relationship, sit back decisively and say, in effect: 'Now you are grown up. You have spent years listening to teachers and reading the Bible. Now let us start at your end. What are the things that worry you? I do not promise to settle all your difficulties. I do promise to bring to bear upon them some considerations that will throw light upon them.'

Starting from this point, the class will be in no doubt of the relevance of what they are doing. We begin here on the right side, without having to climb the wall of uncomprehending that so often stands between us and them in a 'scripture lesson'. They will know that we, though teachers, are concerned about the situation in which they are placed. What may not be so easy to establish is that what we have to say does, palpably and vitally, reach their situation. Some who have read thus far will think of their own classes, and suspect that the whole approach is too difficult for them to follow. We start, in orthodox modern school style, with the concrete; but our method proceeds to make one abstraction after another, and to press on to the supreme abstraction, the concept of God. What can all this mean for the 'dull' child? Is it realistic to ask 4 C to *think* about all this in a systematic way?

We must plainly admit that with some of our pupils we shall make less progress than with others; but that happens in all subjects and with all methods. All may learn a few mathematical tricks, but only a few learn to think mathematically. And it is equally certain that while all can learn a few religious ideas, only a few will learn to think systematically about religious issues.

Yet the attempt must be made, because all must be brought up against the discovery that there *is* such a thing as religious thought, that it is not merely a matter of inherited prejudice, blind faith or wilful scepticism. Further, those who do not think must have an occasion to meet and confront those who do, not only for what they can learn from them, but for what they can offer, from their difficulty, as challenge to the thoughtful. They may learn much from their own thoughtful friends that they could not learn from a teacher. Those who are just seeing the point for themselves are the best instructors of those who are not quite there. Even more effective are those who have seen half the point, and are still debating with the supporters of the other half.

To this end, many teachers have abandoned altogether the ability-grouping or streaming practised in other subjects. They have found this another means of pointing the shift to adult standards. 'Now,' they are implying, 'you are grown up, and we need to discuss adult issues in an adult way. So we are pulling out of the ordinary classroom situation, and are forming working parties to think and talk together.' Some good things are sacrificed: the possibility of pushing a bright group into more difficult fields, or taking a slow group gently over familiar problems in the language of their ordinary conversation. But the loss may be worth the gain: in setting the able to argue together in the presence of the less able, and to draw the slower ones at last into the argument, even if they say nothing more original than 'Yes, yes, I agree with that'.

It will by now be manifest that the rôle of the teacher in this approach is far more exacting than that he is accustomed to fill. Instead of being an exponent, in direct control of the situation, he becomes a contributor exercising the gentlest of control by the most indirect of means. Instead of working outwards from a text or a prepared scheme, he works inwards from novel and unsystematic situations. Instead of netting his fish he must tickle them and hope they will swim in the right direction.

Before he can do this with skill and ease the practised teacher has many habits of mind and feeling to reverse. He is accustomed to maintaining a situation in which class control stems from his own speech and action. Now he must still guarantee order, without himself being in the centre of affairs. He is accustomed to making his points in an order disposed by the logic of the subject. Now he must wait for the points to arise, and must keep one point waiting for another until the opportunity for marking the pattern is clear. He is accustomed to the kind of lesson that can be drawn together and rounded off. Now he must deal with material that may, it is true, draw together, but must then be left open again to all the untidiness of real life.

Many teachers will feel that the whole process is too risky to be undertaken. To them we would suggest that the answer to their anxiety lies in the discovery of a few other teachers in their neighbourhood who are considering this kind of approach, and the formation of a group for study, discussion and preparation. The machinery for forming such a group is already in existence. The Institute of Christian Education has this as one of its tasks; while the local University Institute of Education will often provide a meeting place and guidance in programme planning. Help could also be claimed from local churches, within which both clergy and laity should have a concern for education.

The impetus for such an association might be gained from a conference of representative interests: teachers in both grammar and modern schools, clergy and ministers, laymen in the local churches, the University Institute of Education, men and women in industry, and parents who have shown interest and insight. The general task to be faced at the conference is to describe the moral and personal situation of the adolescent in the region, and to assemble information about the kind of help he is given, at school, at work, at church, in the youth service, to understand his rôle. When this has been achieved, the rest should follow without difficulty. The teachers' group would be able to set out on its task with a knowledge of the broader background of their pupils' lives, and of where to find help on particular issues, theological, social and industrial.

An outline programme could be drawn up from the topics suggested in this book, one or two teachers, initiating a discussion of how the problem could be presented, and at a later meeting several could report on how it went. It would be important, however, to ensure that the group was not exclusively concerned with problems of method. These will most easily be solved by those teachers who enter most fully into the experiences and thought of their pupils, and who are ready to talk about them honestly and simply. In essence, discussion is not a 'method' but a relationship between persons; and it presents difficulties only because the necessary formalities of the classroom demand a measure of aloofness and conventionality, a certain distance, that makes personal relationships to some extent artificial. The formal difficulties, however, will yield to trust and frankness; the distance will vanish when it is once perceived that now the teacher is on the same side as the class, no longer pressing his knowledge upon their ignorance, but offering his experience to their need.

There is here, awaiting us, a new frontier to our whole educational endeavour. We have learnt to stand alongside the grammar school leaver, in the co-operative climate of the sixth form. The modern school has tended to think of its leavers as children. But they are older than we think. It may be the task of the teacher of religion to open for the whole school this frontier of maturity, to find the point at which their boys and girls turn into men and women.

CONCLUSION

THIS study has been concerned with boys and girls who have virtually finished their school career. It has taken them seriously when they say that they find their lessons on the Bible childish and irrelevant. And it has explored ways of setting teenage problems at the centre of things, and enabling puzzled youngsters to talk about what lies nearest to their hearts.

It remains to say a final word on how this last year's work fits into a whole school course. Is this shift from Bible teaching to real-life situations to be recommended for the first three years of the secondary school, or is it to be reserved for the last?

The objections to beginning the problem approach before the last year are many and formidable. Juniors do not feel the sheer weight of the problems we have outlined; they do not view themselves as adults; they are so bound by particular instances that they cannot generalize; they can make isolated points in argument, but they cannot sustain a line of thought. Two special considerations seem to us so powerful as to be decisive. If the shift to discussion is made too soon, there would be no means of facing the leaver with a challenge to adult responsibility. He cannot be told, at the beginning of his last year, 'Now you are grown-up. We are going to start again, in a new way.' And further, if problems are made the centre too soon, the Bible itself will be in danger of being pushed to the perimeter. A four-year programme of ill-informed talk would not constitute a means of religious education.

At the same time, the last year, with its new, adult point of view, needs preparation beforehand. Religious instruction is bound by the same laws as other instruction: there must be continuity and progress, unity and development. While the first three years must continue to be based on the Bible, it will be necessary to begin during that time to view it as a book about the human condition, rather than a book about remote history. The issues with which the Bible deals are perennially fresh and urgent: the nature of man, the choice between taking life seriously and letting it happen, between a large view and a small view of human destiny, the meaning of conscience, and experience of absolute obligation in which men are aware of God.

The detailed narratives of the Exodus and the occupation of Canaan, the reigns of Saul and David and Solomon, are surely of little importance beside the great burden of Old Testament history: that a people who in the perils and bleakness of desert life had become aware of God, were faced by the temptations of luxury and greed, and involved in the shifts and schemes of power politics; that they were broken up by the powers they sought to exploit; and struggled back from exile, aware that the God of History demanded their complete allegiance. In their corporate guilt and fear they refined their laws and regulations, in the vain hope of manufacturing a system that would keep them, morally and ritually, pure; and were held in it, and lost their best vitality. Jesus, born into this freezing tradition, took hold of it, illuminated it, and released the spirit of liberty in which obedience to the will of God became vitalizing and creative, instead of negative and repressive. The forces of fear gathered themselves to destroy him, but they failed, for the love of God broke out through his death, swept out through his risen life into the lives of men, and spread through the world, triumphant again and again, wherever men were faithful.

This is the story of the Bible that must be told before boys and girls can be asked to face for themselves the question, 'What does the love of God mean now?' The selection and ordering of material will vary from school to school, from class to class, from teacher to teacher. It is not important, so long as a coherent picture emerges by the end. The aim is to gain sufficient grasp of the grand argument that the specific problems of today can be set against the essentially timeless statement of the Bible: that modern suffering should be illuminated by the insight of the prophets, Job and the New Testament; that present-day refugees should be viewed in the light of the Old Testament concern for the stranger and Jesus' teaching about our duty to our neighbour; that the waste land of modern life should recall memories of Horeb and the resurgence of Christian hope in the Early Church.

In some such vision of the Bible lies the only hope of restoring it to the place it used to hold, as a book that ordinary men are glad to read. At present it is broadly true to say that the Bible is 'done' in class; but thereafter done with. Yet the aim of scripture teaching is still, as it always was, to make a gift for a life-time, so that men and women facing the problems of living and ageing should have beside them, open to their understanding, the infinite dimensions in which they stand.

A four-year course would thus make two different approaches. For the first three years, the Bible would provide the themes, historical moral and spiritual, pressed as far as may be towards the contemporary historical, moral and spiritual situation. In the last, the present world, as immediately experienced by our young people, would provide the themes, which would be pressed back to the Bible where these same themes were originally, and so profoundly, explored.

If the work is well done, the young adult will take into his new life something in which he must believe and by which he must stand.

APPENDICES

FIVE LESSONS ON THE CHRISTIAN VIEW OF SEX AND MARRIAGE

TEACHERS will be interested in this first-hand account of a series of lessons on sex and marriage conducted by Mrs Hills Cotterill at Kidbrooke School. They are attached to the syllabus in religious education, with the full concurrence of the Head of the Department for Science, on the grounds that the information on reproduction in the science course should not be linked with the human problems of marriage and family life.

The lessons are known to be available. Any department teacher can make side reference to them, and draw the question, 'What lessons? Can we have them?' The general purpose of the lessons is then outlined, without detail, and the class is given time to decide among themselves if they wish to have them. They are then told that arrangements will have to be made with the Head of the Department of Religious Education and classes changed over between teachers. Then a date is arranged by which time the class may expect its course to begin. All this impresses on them the importance the staff attach to this work and the sincerity it demands from the pupils.

Lesson 1 (Genesis 1.27—8; 2.7, 18, 24).

An introduction along the following lines: 'You have asked for these lessons and we have put ourselves out to provide them for you. Your full co-operation is what I now count upon. There will be no problems of discipline because we are behaving in a grown-up way and doing something vital together. Nobody need talk if she cannot contribute sincerely; anyone may say anything that is on the point, with no holds barred. I am never shocked by anything to do with sex, good or bad, so you need not be shocked either. Adult life means living in sex relationships with others, husband, children, family life.'

The material then presented varies with every class and with each time of giving the lesson, but covers this general ground: 'Sex is part of God's creative work. He made all things good, including sex. He could plan no better way by which human souls come into fellowship with themselves than through the experience of love and self-giving which true marriage implies. God is not male or female: some non-Christian faiths use male and female deities; but to the Christian God is both; he is either or neither. It is important to avoid the notion that God is *above* sex, indifferent or superior to it. The "image of God" means many things, but includes in it somewhere the male-female experience which is normal to us. You are in some ways incomplete until you have found completion with the right man: not just sexual completion but marriage. You and I, women, have a unique part to play in this matter, as "helps meet" for man, as complements, partners.' The problem of equality between the sexes may come up here and be briefly discussed, with the note that we shall meet it later and perhaps can think more about it before making sweeping statements.

Lesson 2 (Psalm 8).

How we were made—drawing together what has been learnt of the physical aspect of sex in science lessons. They usually like to have it re-taught: menstruation, moods and headaches that sometimes go with this, religious excitements that sweep over them in the middle teens—'My pin-up boys are Liberace and Billy Graham.' They sometimes ask about school-girl 'pashes' and homosexuality. Self-abuse they never mention, but once I gave them figures for the prevalence of what I called 'private bad-habits' as the situation seemed to demand some reference to it. I give some details of the difference between boys and girls. Boys have no menstruation, but have other problems. There is the analogy of the penny-farthing bicycle to illustrate the difference in feeling: the boy, the small wheel, quickly moved and short in range, the sex experience at white heat and then all over; the girl, the large wheel, slower to move and with a longer range, physical excitement passing into childbirth and home. Petting comes up, from them, in the form, 'How far can I let him go?' [1] 'Why can't we have a good time together if he promises to marry me?' is another chestnut. I try to teach respect for each other as whole persons, not just as bodies capable of stimulation.

Lesson 3 (Mark 10.1-9, esp. 7, 8).

How old ought a girl to be when she marries? Except for one case of a retarded fifteen-year-old I have always found the girls firmly of the opinion that a girl who marries under eighteen, or even twenty-one, is a fool. They often fail to link marriage with the material of the previous lesson. Marriage is 'for love', granted, but other factors weigh heavily: job, wages, home, good time, children. What do you look for, then, in the boy who may one day be the home-maker? Their suggestions are all the usual ones, and show great good sense: humour, good temper, good looks, ability to earn a decent living. Then we go on: what about tastes? Do you want to marry someone who shares yours or are you prepared to learn to like his? Church-going is often raised, and the problem of mixed marriages, Jew and Christian, Christian and Mormon, white and coloured. Social class difficulties do not occur to them, and when I raise them they dismiss them. 'Why shouldn't the duchess marry her chauffeur? He's as good as she is!' They do not know, and find it hard to grasp, that marriage is a way of life and not just an occurrence. Boredom after

[1] Rose Hacker's book, *Telling the Teenager,* has forthright chapters on shallow and deep petting for those who need strong meat.

some years of marriage crops up, and I recommend David Mace's *The Art of Marriage* which is also helpful on the frequently mentioned dread of the 'other woman' once the girl has lost her looks in running the home and minding the children.

Lesson 4 (Matthew 19.3-15).

Divorce. You think you have found the right young man. You have behaved yourselves and have a right to a 'white wedding'. We read over the relevant portions of the marriage service. Should marriage vows be permanent or for a trial period? Most girls go for permanence as providing the best challenge to endeavour. The honeymoon is negotiated with love and mutual thoughtfulness. The 'art of marriage' has been pondered and you are ready to do all that lies in your power to be a good and attractive wife.

Then what goes wrong? I use here the difficult verses 10-12; frigidity, withdrawal of one from the other over fancied or real hurts, resentments, jealousies. We use Ephesians 5.1-5; loose talk leading to loose ideas and 'flirting with the lodger, the insurance man'. We discuss the kind of self-discipline which avoids films and plays and television shows that induce a soft attitude to sin. I mention the prevalent women's magazine silly serial: 'She did wrong but what would YOU have done in her place?'

Lesson 5.

A review. What loose threads have we left untied? Many, always, but I let them say what they want to hear more on and to ask extra questions. A.I.D. appears, and the new contraceptive pill. They often note that we have only just begun to get things straight. I agree. Can they have some more talks? I will consider this, for now they have much to think over.

At term end, or for weekly prep, they do essays, without names, discussing their ideas or feelings about a number of topics touched on.

Books

Books for their use or for the teacher to read:

Mace, David, *The Art of Marriage* (Fontana)
Capper and Williams, *Heirs Together* (IVF)
Valentine, C. W., *The Normal Child* (Pelican)
    Moral Problems (Mowbray)
ed. Hayes, E. H., *Over to You* (REP)
Kerr, Colin, *The Bulwarks of a Nation* (MMS)
Reed, B. H., *For Teenagers Only* (Epworth)
Warren, H. C., *Sex Education Booklets* (SCM Press)
Hood, F., *Talks to Girls* (Mothers' Union)
    Human Relationships (GFS leaflets)
Barnes, K. C., *He and She* (Darwen Finlayson)
    (from the boy's angle)

BIBLIOGRAPHY

Books for Pupils

The Bible, Revised Standard Version, (School ed., Nelson)
Farrar, A., *A Shorter Bible* (Fontana)
Fanchiotti, M., *A Beginner's Bible* (OUP)
ed. Hayes, E. H., *Begin Here!* and *Over to You* (REP)
Walton, R., *What Do Christians Really Believe?* (SCM Press)
Titterton and Firth, *The End of the Roads* (Ginn)
Platten, T. G., *The Living Faith,* Book 4 (ULP)
Thinking Things Through booklets (SCM Press)

Books for Teachers

Avery, M., *Religious Education in the Modern School* (REP)
     „   *Teaching Scripture* (REP)
Phillips, J. B., *New Testament Christianity* (Hodder)
     „   *Your God is too Small* (Epworth)
Ramsey, I., *Religious Language* (SCM Press)
Dodd, C. H., *The Bible To-day* (CUP)
Lewis, C. S., *The Problem of Pain* (Bles)
Niblett, W. R., *Education and the Modern Mind* (Faber)
     „   *Christian Education in a Secular Society* (OUP)
Neil, W., *The Re-discovery of the Bible* (Hodder)
MacIntyre, A., *Difficulties in Christian Belief* (SCM Press)
Youngman-Hulton, B., *Teaching Religious Knowledge* (ULP)
Williams, M. S., *Scripture in Class* (REP)
Caird, G. B., *The Truth of the Gospel* (OUP)
Williams, J. G., *Worship and the Modern Child* (SPCK)
Bowley and Townroe, *The Spiritual Development of the Child* (E. and
                              S. Livingstone)

MEMBERS OF THE STUDY GROUP

D. G. O. Ayerst, H.M.I.
Miss B. M. Bray, Headmistress, John Pounds Secondary Modern School
for Girls, Portsea
Miss J. Briddon, Headmistress, Bexleyheath County Secondary School
for Girls.
Mrs J. Hills Cotterill, Scripture Specialist, Kidbrooke School, S.E. 3
C. W. Gardiner, Headmaster, Intake County Secondary School, Leeds
Miss E. M. Johnson, Adviser in Children's Work, London Diocesan
Council for Voluntary Religious Education
The Rev L. P. Smith, Culham College
The Rev R. C. Walton, Schools Broadcasting Department, B.B.C.

A. E. Williams, Headmaster, Archbishop Temple's C. of E. Secondary Boys' School, S.E. 1

The Rev E. C. F. Bache, Executive Officer, Institute of Christian Education, *Secretary*

Harold Loukes, Reader in Education, University of Oxford, *Chairman*

APPENDIX D

SCHOOLS CO-OPERATING IN THE STUDY

Schools used for Tape-recordings

> Intake County Secondary School, Leeds (Mixed)
> Penwortham Secondary Modern School, Lancs (Boys)
> John Pounds Secondary Modern School, Portsea (Girls)
> Radcliffe County Secondary School, Lancs (Boys)
> Kidbrooke School (Girls)
> Headington County Secondary School, Oxford (Mixed)

Schools used for Questionnaires

All the above, and in addition

> Priory Secondary Girls' School, Isle of Wight
> Oxford Street Secondary Boys' School, Swansea
> Aberconwy Secondary School, Conway (Mixed)
> South Wigston Secondary Modern School for Boys, Leicester
> High School, Withernsea (Mixed)
> Marton Grove Secondary Girls' School, Middlesborough
> Huntley Secondary Boys' School, Tunbridge Wells
> Archbishop Temple's Boys' Secondary School, Lambeth

The number of questionnaires completed varied from school to school between 20 and 50, making a total of 502.

APPENDIX D

THE COMMENTARIES

The material on which chapter II is based was gathered from written statements made in class. Teachers were asked to explain the general intention of the study, and to assure their pupils that they could write as freely and sincerely as they pleased. The text on which comments were invited follows in full.

PLEASE READ THIS CAREFULLY

Here is a collection of remarks that have been made by boys and girls of your own age and in a number of schools.

We ask you to think about them now. Decide whether you agree or

disagree with what is said. Then write down your views in a sentence or two in the spaces provided.
Do not write your name.
Do say what you honestly think.

1. The Bible

'The Bible's not forced to be true, we don't know ourselves that it's true. It could be something that's been made up quite a long time ago since.'

2. God made the world

'Well, it could be true, Miss, but it's not proved, is it? Nobody stood there and watched him, so we don't know if he did it or not.'

3. Jesus Christ

'I think Jesus Christ was just an ordinary man—after all, he came down in the form of a man. I think he was just a very clever man that came on earth before his time, because nowadays by an operation you can make blind people see again.'

4. God

'I've always imagined God as an old man with long hair and a beard, wearing white robes, with a nice calm face and that.'

5. Lessons on the Bible

'Well, I think as we grew older they were still telling us the same kind of things, instead of more adultish things.'

6. Is Christianity worth dying for?

'Well, what good would I be shot? I mean, I couldn't do much good in the world shot, so I might as well carry on living.'
'I don't know what good Jesus did dying on the Cross.'

7. Is it boring to be good?

On the whole, do you prefer to be made *to be good, or do you prefer to be allowed to be bad if you want?*
'I'd rather be bad.'
And are you prepared to take the consequence of being bad?
'Yes.'
'Well, it would be ever so dull with everybody being good and cheerful and so on. It changes the routine if somebody is bad once in a while.'
'You have to be a bit cheeky to get on, anyway.'

8. Is there a heaven?

'I'd say there's a heaven if you believe in Jesus, but there's a heaven because you think you're going to Jesus, but if you've never believed in Jesus, then you don't know where you're going.'
'Well, I don't think there's a place like heaven. I think that you kind of come back into the world again, to live and lead a better life, and you go on coming back until you're perfect, and then, well there isn't a place, but I think you go to God when you're perfect. When you're fit to go to him.'

9. Is it fair of God to allow suffering?

'God couldn't care for us, or else he would stop all accidents and all suffering, murders and things like that.'

10. *Is prayer any use?*

'I like it when we pray for the sick. I think that something really happens when you pray for the sick people and the old people.'

11. *Going to church*

'Every church has the same atmosphere—a dead atmosphere.'
'I don't like going to Church because there aren't any people of my own age there. I don't think I'd be welcome.'

12. *What sort of Scripture lessons would you like?*

'There's too much thinking done for you.'
'Yes, it's much more interesting when you can discuss than just be taught.'

13. *Religion and everyday life*

'All they preach about is Christ's life—that's basic Christianity, granted, but it does not preach about something that's going to happen, something to look forward to, to give the young people something to base their religion on.'

INDEX